Better Homes and Gardens

Celebrate

Volume 6

contents

summer

92 Sunshiny, glorious flag-waving days of summer beckon with new crafting techniques to set your spirits soaring. Super-creative pillows, planters, and more stylishly usher in the season. As a salute to repurposing, discover new uses for discarded books and vases.

boo!

118 Creepy, crawly, and a whole lot of fun, Halloween is one holiday for your imagination to run wild. Give in to fiendish instincts with spooktacular ideas that set your home apart this haunting season. And when ghouls come knocking, you'll have the best treats in town.

easy does it

Here's our little bonus: These ingenious projects are easy and economical.

- pin spin *page 30*
- seed packets *page 62*
- crostini *page 90*
- book nook *page 116*
- frightful favors *page 152*

Meredith Consumer Marketing
Consumer Marketing Product Director: Heather Sorensen
Consumer Marketing Product Manager: Wendy Merical
Consumer Marketing Billing/Renewal Manager: Tami Beachem
Business Director: Ron Clingman
Senior Production Manager: Al Rodruck

Waterbury Publications, Inc.
Editorial Director: Lisa Kingsley
Creative Director: Ken Carlson
Associate Editors: Tricia Bergman, Mary Williams
Associate Design Director: Doug Samuelson
Production Assistant: Mindy Samuelson
Contributing Editor: Sue Banker
Contributing Copy Editor: Peg Smith
Contributing Proofreader: Linda Wagner

Better Homes and Gardens® Magazine
Editor in Chief: Stephen Orr
Executive Editor: Oma Blaise Ford
Managing Editor: Gregory H. Kayko
Creative Director: Michael D. Belknap
Senior Deputy Editor, Food and Entertaining: Nancy Wall Hopkins

Meredith National Media Group
President: Tom Harty

Meredith Corporation
Chairman and Chief Executive Officer: Stephen M. Lacy

In Memoriam: E.T. Meredith III (1933–2003)

Make It Extraordinary

Isn't it wonderful when a dinner party is a success due to your winning menu? How fun is it when you make someone's day with a personalized handcrafted gift? And how good do you feel surrounded by decor that lets your personality shine? All those feel-good moments truly put the *happy* into our lives.

Better Homes and Gardens® Celebrate, Volume 6, helps you amp up ingenuity to make the most of your days, surroundings, and relationships. From tried-and-true recipes that turn any day of the week into a special occasion to DIY projects that transform your home into a place to cherish, *Celebrate* is packed with ways to make it happen.

And let's remember the party ideas! Follow our lead and you'll be awarded accolades by family and friends. Whether it's a birthday party, holiday, or casual gathering, *Celebrate* offers loads of ideas to ensure memorable times together.

Speaking of time, we keep minutes in mind as well as dollars. There are ideas that are easy on time and money. From the first day of the new year to that fun-filled

night of bats, cats, and costumes, *Celebrate* helps you craft, cook, and concoct.

So go ahead—put on your creativity cap and make every day special for you and those you love. We'll be your silent sidekick, showing you how every step of the way.

Here's to extraordinary days ahead,

Sue Barker

LET THE YEAR
begin

GOOD THINGS AHEAD

Get the new year off to a good start with creative
party ideas and amazing decorating options.

Resolution Tree

Accomplish New Year's resolutions then display the written reminders on an artful tree.

Leaves of Promise

Write self-oaths on paper leaves, then attach to the tree when each goal is achieved or a task completed.

WHAT YOU'LL NEED
tracing paper
pencil
scissors
12-inch square of black and white patterned scrapbook paper
scrapbook paper in desired colors for leaves
13½×10½-inch sheet of neutral scrapbook paper for background
glue stick
black marking pen
13½×10½-inch frame
jar

WHAT YOU DO
1. Trace the tree and leaf patterns, page 155, onto tracing paper. Cut out patterns.
2. Fold the black and white scrapbook paper in half. Use the pattern to trace the tree shape; cut out. Use the leaf pattern to cut approximately 50 leaves from assorted scrapbook papers.
3. Unfold the tree. Center and glue onto the neutral background paper. Remove the glass from the frame. Glue the tree paper to the backing insert then secure in frame.
4. Use the marking pen to write different resolutions on each leaf. Fold leaves in half lengthwise. Set aside extra leaves to write on as the year progresses.
5. Place resolution leaves in the jar. As goals are achieved or tasks completed, randomly glue the leaves to the tree branches.

Snapshot Birthday Bash

Whatever the date, whatever the age, these personalized photo decorations are one creative way to share loving birthday wishes.

Gather 'Round

What could be better than being surrounded by family and friends on your birthday? Combine photos of others amongst photos of the honoree. To let the guest of honor shine, mat a few photos to draw special attention to him or her. Choose a color palette and let it shine using coordinating wrapping paper as a tablerunner.

Card of Thanks

Reproduce a party photo into a thank-you card. Whether printed at home or a store, photos add a personal touch to any thank you. For parties for little ones, include the birthday girl's or boy's parents in the photo, so the thanks come from the entire family.

Place Card Pic

Check flea markets, garage sales, and antiques stores for old cameras of all styles. Non-working cameras can usually be picked up inexpensively. They add to the theme, prop up decorations, and are perfect bases to hold photo place cards. To make place cards, use a tag punch to cut out a photo of each guest then adhere to white cardstock using glue stick; trim a narrow border. Tie the tag to a camera with ribbon.

Top That

Designate which dessert belongs to the birthday boy or girl by planting his or her pic into the sweet treat. Simply punch out a circular head shot and back with a slightly larger solid color circle; glue a toothpick between the layers. To amp up details, add a paper hat trimmed with glittery pom-poms.

Too-Cute Confetti

Home-printed photos, cut into circles, make super-fun confetti. Dress up those of the birthday boy or girl with frames of colorful paper, ribbon bows, and paper triangle hats topped with pom-pom trims. Toss in scrapbook paper circles to add to the festive tabletop.

The Gang's All Here

Show the birthday honoree some smiles! Simply back photo confetti with a second layer of paper and glue with a wire through the center. Attach ends to the hands of a doll-size mannequin for a mini garland.

Meaningful Wrap

Output photos on printer paper to make super-special birthday wrap. If the birthday honoree is in the photo, create a call-out with a scrapbook-paper hat.

Let the Year **Begin**

Play By Play

Draw football diagrams on chalkboard paper for an easy runner or banner. For a cheer-y centerpiece, fill a super tall trophy vase (from a party rental store) with DIY pom-poms.

First Down
SEVEN LAYER DIP

Point After
PRETZELS

Line of Scrimmage
SANDWICHES

Super Party

Hosting a get-together for the big game? Score big with this playbook for sure-to-win decorations and easy eats.

Cocktails and Coasters

Mix up a signature drink for the game. Pair it with chipboard coasters made with number stencils.

Game on Game

Up game-day fun with computer-printed bingo cards. Instead of only covering up numbers, include symbols seen on TV. Keep shiny whistles on hand to announce winning cards.

Holding Penalty

Five-layer dip in single-serving cups keeps noshing casual and prevents penalties for double dipping.

Sideline Sandwiches

Order a mix of deli sandwiches for sure-to-please fare. Food label tents define the play. If several choices are offered, include ingredients on labels.

Little Ideas, Lotsa Love

Show your Valentine oodles of affection with clever surprises made with a whole lot of heart.

Double Duty

Surprise your sweetie with a mini bouquet that nests in a clear drinking glass brushed with liquid gold leaf for glam. Include a second glass to make a set. When flowers fade, use the glasses to toast with your forever Valentine.

Key to My Heart Art

Create focal-point art centered around a gold-painted key. Two empty flea-market frames, united with coats of fresh white paint, shine a spotlight on this symbol of love.

Happy Squiggles

Express your inner lovebird with free-form word art. Drop thick natural-fiber rope into a mixture of 1½ cups warm water, 1 cup flour, 1 cup cornstarch, 1 cup crafts glue, and 1 teaspoon salt. Shape the rope into the word "love" and a heart frame, layering the design on a piece of plastic wrap as you work. The rope should harden within 24 hours. When dry and hardened, tack the lettering on a wall. Attach decorative birds or other embellishments with hot glue.

Get It Together

Clever and showy, these paint-trimmed household helpers get you organized for the year ahead.

Unjumbled Jewels

Add a pinch of pizzazz to the inside of drawers with patterned adhesive shelf liner. A light background helps to show off contents of the drawer. For jewelry, coins, or other small objects, dress up dollar-store food containers using a small paintbrush to coat the rim and underside with crafts paint. To find items in a jiffy, use paint colors to differentiate groupings.

Color Coded

Bring color and order to your wardrobe by painting the fronts and backs of natural wood hangers with crafts paint. Let the paint dry. Seal the painted hangers with polyurethane to prevent the color from rubbing onto fabric. Designate specific colors to organize garments by person, size, season, or clothing type.

Pencil It In

Keep art tools close at hand for moments of inspiration.
Wrap a decorative cup or small planter with painter's tape
to create a straight painting edge. Apply crafts paint; let
dry. Paint a second coat and carefully remove the tape.
When dry, spray the container with clear topcoat and let
dry. To cushion the bottom of the container, cut a circle of
cork to fit then glue in place.

Mine, Yours, Ours

Put spray paint to work on highly textured surfaces—it's
the best medium for conquering hard-to-reach areas, such
as the crevices in a woven basket. Cheerful stripes, applied
in a straight line thanks to painter's tape, perk up neutral
storage bins. Use different colors to assign baskets to
family members—a trick that works for all ages, even for
pre-readers.

Luck of the Irish

Host a St. Patrick's Day party with a bit of the green that works up as quick as a leprechaun's shenanigans.

Pick Your Favorite

Let lucky guests take home a little green. Pair foliage fronds with delicate clear glass vases for quick, yet striking, party favors.

Napkin Tag

Fern-motif stamps make it easy to add a detailed frond to tags. Press the stamp onto a green ink pad then onto a paper tag; let dry. Lace each stamped tag with leather cording then drape over a napkin.

Posy Under Glass

Turn a few humble stems into an impressive centerpiece. Pop them into a short stemmed glass then cover with a cloche. A simple palette of green and white keeps the St. Paddy's Day theme crisp.

Color Splash

Bid adieu to winter with home accents that are inspired by vivid color.

Bright Spot

Decorator fabrics offer color choices to inspire fresh decor. Choose a fairly heavy weave to use for several projects. Tie in coordinating fabrics and ribbons to add interest to the mix that stays with or complements the color scheme.

In Stitches

Fabric, stretched over artist's canvas, brings favorite colors and patterns to the wall. For added interest, machine-stitch on the fabric. For dark stitching, choose fabric that incorporates mostly light to mid tones. For light stitching, darker print fabrics work best. For this floral fabric, we stitched straight stems (several times to achieve a prominent look) with circular flowers at the top. You can outline fabric motifs, stitch patterns, or simply stitch randomly over the fabric. To stitch a border, use a pencil and ruler to draw a guide a couple inches smaller than the canvas. Stitch around the border several times for a border approximately 1 inch wide.

Soft Touch

A clear glass cylinder gets a pretty facelift with a strip of fabric flanked by ribbons. To adhere the pieces to the vase, first glue the fabric strip slightly below center. Using low-temp glue, adhere one end in place, wrap the vase and overlap ends; glue. Repeat with each ribbon length.

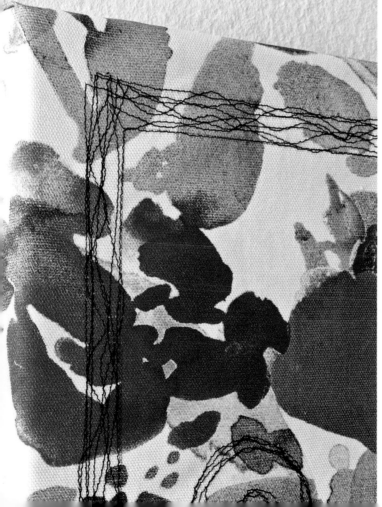

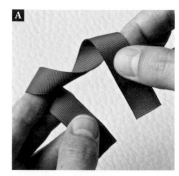

Cheery Welcome

This everlasting wreath blooms with color and texture and can be enjoyed until holiday decorations appear at year's end. To make the greenery, cut 6-inch lengths from several types of green ribbon; knot in center. Hot-glue knots to a flat wreath form, placing in varying directions as shown, opposite. For dark green ribbon accents, twist ribbon as shown in Photo A. Hot-glue ribbon ends together; glue to wreath. Add in a few blue knotted ribbons, see Photo B. For roses, use 2-inch-wide patterned wired ribbon. Cut an 18-inch length, gathering one side by pulling on wire as shown in Photo C. Pattern to inside, wrap ribbon around itself as shown in Photo D. Use pulled wire to tightly wrap base of rose as shown in Photo E; hot-glue to wreath.

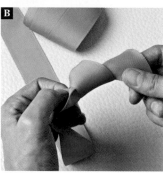

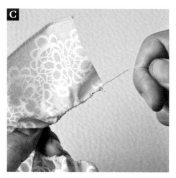

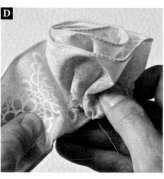

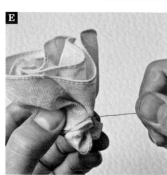

Plate Place

Decorative mesh rolls, available in crafts and fabric stores, offer myriad color options for place mats. Choose mesh that coordinates with your color scheme then cut to placemat size. Fray all edges. Choose three coordinating ribbons, like those shown, and cut to fit the placemat. Fold one ribbon in half lengthwise; machine-stitch it to the left side of place mat. Overlap the first ribbon with a second then stitch using several rows of wavy stitching. Repeat for third ribbon.

Napkin Nicety

Ribbon and fabric make stylish color-coordinated napkin rings. For each ring, cut a 2¼×8-inch strip of fabric. Fold under ½ inch along each long edge; press. Place the fabric strip in the center of an 8-inch length of 3-inch-wide ribbon. Machine-stitch wavy lines along center of fabric. Fold under ¼ inch on one end of fabric-topped ribbon; hand stitch ends together.

Landing Pad

Use fabric scraps to make pretty coasters. For each, cut a square slightly smaller than a square cork coaster. Carefully pull threads from edges to fringe. Machine-stitch as for the wall piece (page 25) if desired. Use waterproof spray glue to attach fabric to cork.

Pin Spin

Say It With Meaning

Word stamps transform plain clothespins into mini messengers. Simply dab small stamps onto an ink pad then press onto a clothespin. Use the message carriers to close lunch bags, attach to notes, snap onto napkins, or clip wherever you want to share a positive thought with friends or family.

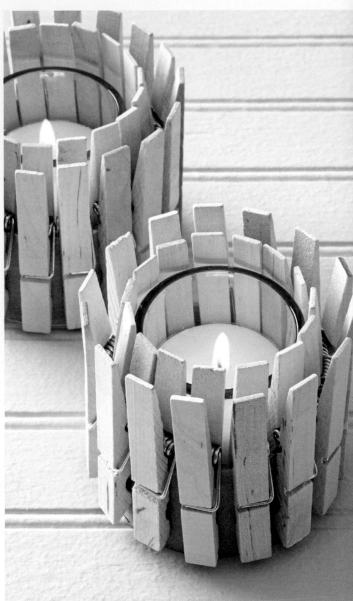

Natural Light

Short cans, such as those from tuna, are just the right height to clip on clothespins. Cover the entire can then set a glass votive inside to protect the clothespins from flame. Never leave candles burning unattended.

Pattern Play

Patterned clothespins, available in crafts and scrapbooking stores, lend a fresh look to a wreath. Using a flat wreath form for the base, hot-glue clothespins in a color pattern or randomly. Use various size pins to add interest to the shape.

Magnetic Personality

Choose a color scheme by gluing strips of patterned paper to one side of clothespins. Slip out one wood section of clothespin. Use glue stick to hold paper in place, pressing into crevice for wire. Reassemble clothespin. Cut a piece of adhesive-backed magnet to fit the back of the clothespin then press in place. Use the clips on refrigerators, metal filing cabinets, or message boards.

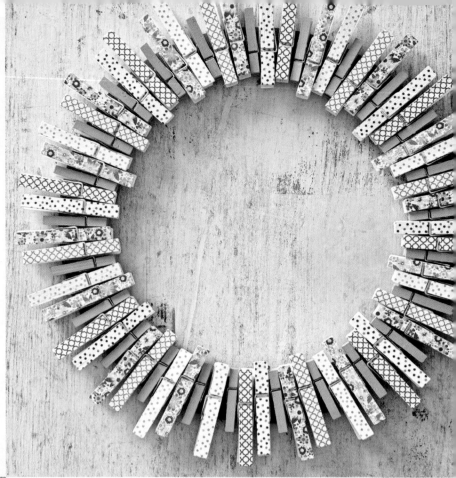

At the Table

Make mini easels to hold place cards. For each holder, hot-glue pairs of clothespins together, aligning ends to stand upright. Cut a 1×3½-inch piece of patterned paper, adding a small strip of white for name. Write name on strip. Cut a 1½×4-inch piece of white cardstock. Clip the white paper onto the back two clothespins and the patterned piece on the front two clothespins. Slip in a sprig of greenery for a fresh touch.

GOOD VIBES

spring

THE SEASON IN BLOOM

As the earth reawakens, enjoy all the beauty and happiness that spring holds. This chapter offers a bouquet of ideas to make the most of get-togethers, yard facelifts, and room revamps.

Spring Cues

Create aah-so-simple spring centerpieces with early bloomers and repurposed containers.

Nod to Nature

Tuck in earthy knickknacks, like these faux ceramic fungi, for a woodsy appeal. Inspired by galvanized gutters, this trough planter adds to naturally shabby chic decor.

Box Stars

Fillers, such as spikemoss, act as the supporting cast for seasonal flowers. After blooms fade, foliage carries on this trunk show.

Shed the Light

Repurpose a lantern into a botanical curiosity. "Plant" a small pot of flowers in the candleholder then form a nest with spin-dried grass to conceal the pot.

Clearly Earthy

Sprout fresh wheatgrass in a decked-out glass beaker and let tulips stand tall in a glass cylinder with moss wrapped around the soil.

Spring

Pretty Pastels

Why give eggs all the attention? Deck out an Easter table in vibrant spring hues, mixing patterns for an extra-punchy spread. Little details, like clay pot saucer coasters, mix-and-match lanterns, and make-it-yourself seed packet place cards, add flair.

Easter Day Hues

Guests will hop for joy to this pretty table that beckons Easter celebration.

Petal Power

Set an Easter table with pure flower power. Call on bouquets of grocery store blooms and floral napkins cut from fabric remnants. For favors, float flower heads in clear glass dessert cups or shallow candleholders. Large glass candle lanterns add elegance while a long inexpensive scarf in hot pink brightens the party table.

Good Eggs

Go ahead! Hatch a fresh new way to decorate with egg techniques that feel like kids' play.

So Easy Eggs

No need to scramble for Easter egg ideas. Hatch up a beautiful batch of patterned eggs using food dye and everyday household materials—kitchen string, electrical tape, and rubber cement. The technique is simple: Apply, dye, remove, and dry. Repeat steps using different color dye for a variation of hues. And here's a tip: Use brown eggs for darker, moodier hues.

Simply Sponged

Pour a small amount of rubber cement into a plastic or paper bowl. Lightly press a sponge into rubber cement to coat. Gently dab sponge on a white or pastel-dyed hard-boiled egg. Set aside for 10 minutes. Dip the sponged egg into a hot dye bath, then spoon over color to achieve the desired shade. Remove egg from the bath and pat dry with a paper towel. While egg is still warm, remove rubber cement by rolling it off the egg with your finger. If desired, add gold speckles to dyed eggs by lightly pressing the sponge into a small amount of gold crafts paint. Gently dab paint onto half the egg; set aside to dry for 15 to 20 minutes. Turn egg over and repeat process on the opposite side.

Totally Tattooed

Trim edges of metallic "flash jewelry" tattoo. Remove the plastic film and place tattoo face down on a dyed hard-boiled egg. Pat the back of the tattoo with a damp—not wet—paper towel. Wait a few seconds, then peel off the paper. If necessary, gently press down any loose edges to seal. Let dry completely before handling.

Lacy Wrap Star

Cut a piece of lace trim just long enough to encircle an egg then place on a flat surface covered with scrap paper. Using a mini sponge paint applicator, apply an even coat of crafts paint to the lace. Quickly transfer lace, paint side up, onto a stack of paper towels then lightly and gently roll egg over the trim, being careful not to touch the wet paint on the egg. Set the lace-patterned egg aside to dry. To change paint colors, rinse the lace in cold water and press onto paper towel until most of the moisture is removed from the lace.

Walls with Wow

Whatever your decorating style, these trendy home wall accents, using your very favorite hues, will fit right in.

A Cut Above

Make your own art for just a few dollars. Dip a variety of veggies into crafts paint and stamp onto mat board. Create your own designs as you go—overlapping or applying symmetrically.

Pipe Dreams

Get your groove on with 3-D abstract art crafted from slices of PVC pipe. Use PVC stain dye to color the pipe. Then randomly dry-brush strokes of acrylic paint onto an artists canvas. Let dry then glue stained slices of PVC pipe to canvas, arranging in any design and slipping smaller-diameter segments inside larger ones for added dimension.

Spring

Clip Art

Rotate art and inspiration swatches with ease when you employ clipboards to frame your latest crushes. Embrace the rustic beauty of standard brown pressed-particle clipboards, which are readily available at office supply stores, or up the glam factor by spray-painting boards a room-coordinating hue and clips a metallic gold.

Pixilated Wall Art

WHAT YOU'LL NEED
20×24-inch stretched artists canvas
pencil and acrylic ruler
acrylic paints in red, green, blue, black, and white
one pad of heavyweight art paper suitable for
    acrylic paint
small paintbrush
paper trimmer
glue stick
clear acrylic spray sealer

WHAT YOU DO
1. Use a pencil and ruler to lightly mark a ½-inch grid on stretched artists canvas.
2. Use the pattern on page 154 as a color guide and for paper placement.
3. Working with one paint color at a time and referring to color key on the pattern, mix paint colors to match colors on key. Paint each color on a separate sheet of heavyweight art paper. Let dry. *Note:* Add small amount of white or black to red, green, and blue to vary colors.
4. Using paper trimmer, cut each paper into ½-inch squares.
5. Following the pattern, use a glue stick to adhere paint squares to each square on canvas.
6. Spray with clear acrylic sealer.

Cinco de Mayo Style

Serve up fun for this holiday with colorful party accents.

Wrapped in Rope

Add modern flair with rope and paint. First, gather a terra-cotta flowerpot, jute rope, hot-glue gun and glue sticks, a paintbrush, and latex paint as shown in Photo A. Place a 2-inch-long bed of hot glue along the bottom edge of the flowerpot. Quickly press the rope into the glue, holding it in place a few seconds until glue hardens slightly. Work in 2-inch segments to ensure the rope bonds to the pot before the glue dries. Continue the process, moving up the container. Place each layer of rope as close to the previous as possible, gluing rope to both the pot and the previous layer as shown in Photo B. Create a band of color by painting several rows of rope with latex paint as shown in Photo C. Add a second coat of paint if necessary.

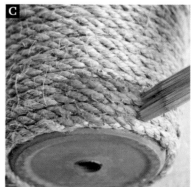

Give 'Em the Slip

Celebrate Cinco de Mayo with a colorful set of embroidered felt coasters that cleverly help party guests identify their glasses. The two-layer coaster slips around a wineglass or margarita glass base through the opening in the top layer and stays on with every sip. To make a coaster, draw a 4-inch circle on two pieces of felt; set one aside for coaster bottom. Using a water-soluble marking pen, trace a ½-inch center square onto the remaining felt circle. Using the corners of the square as guides, draw an X through it. Cut along the drawn lines on the felt circle and cut out center square to make coaster top. Adhere pom-pom trim with fabric glue to the outside edge of the coaster bottom, overlapping trim ends; let dry. Using six strands of embroidery floss for all stitches, stitch French knots, running stitches, cross-stitches, or other stitch around coaster top about ¼ inch from edge. Wrong side up, run a narrow line of fabric glue around the edge of coaster bottom. Place coaster top wrong side down on top of coaster bottom. Let dry.

Clearly Colorful

Sun shines through melted transparent plastic beads,
illuminating the brilliant hues.

Blooms in Blue

Embellish vases with bands of color. To make stripes, place
transparent pony beads on a metal pan, arranging them in the
width of the vase and as wide as desired. For interest, make
two stripes using the same color arrangement with a third
solid stripe to go between. Melt in a 400 degree oven until
fairly flat. For added texture, place a few more beads on top
and return to oven for 5 minutes. Remove from oven and run
under cool water. When dry, use dots of clear glue to attach the
stripes to the vase. To make flowers, place six pony beads
around a contrasting center bead. Melt in the oven until beads
are melted together. Place an additional bead in the center and
return to the oven for 5 minutes. Complete in the same
manner as for the stripes, above.

Spring

Fun Catchers

Metal rings make sturdy molds for brilliant suncatchers. To make each disk, place a ring on a flat cookie sheet. These discs, ranging from 3 to 5 inches in diameter, hold a single color plus clear beads. Fill the ring with translucent tri or pony beads, allowing some spaces around edge. Melt in a 400 degree oven until the beads are fairly flat. Remove from oven and run cool water over tray and plastic. If plastic falls out of ring, carefully adhere together using a few drops of clear instant glue; let dry. To hang, thread cord or elastic thread through a hole near the edge of the ring.

Sunshine Coasters

Colorful, creative, and functional, these one-of-a-kind coasters will brighten up outdoor dining.

WHAT YOU'LL NEED

transparent tri or pony beads
disposable pie plate (patterned bottom, optional)
round cookie or biscuit cutter
oven
plastic adhesive bumper pads

WHAT YOU DO

1. Place the cookie cutter on the pie plate. One with a pattern in the bottom will transfer the pattern to the plastic, adding to the reflective pattern.

2. Arrange a single layer of beads in the cookie cutter. Add a second layer over any gaps as shown in Photo A.

3. Preheat the oven to 400 degrees. Open the windows in the kitchen and surrounding rooms.

4. Carefully place the pie plate in the oven. Melt approximately 20 minutes or until plastic is melted into a smooth sheet as shown in Photo B.

5. Run cold water over the pie plate and melted plastic. Remove cookie cutter as shown in Photo C.

6. Place four clear plastic bumpers on the bottom of the coaster to prevent scratching surfaces.

Food Fetcher

This feeder is mesmerizing even before birds perch. Fill a pizza pan with a double layer of transparent pony beads. Melt in a 400 degree oven until flat. Sprinkle edge with beads; melt until adhered. Run under water; remove. Center disc on an inverted metal bowl, textured edge up. Place in oven. When plastic starts to melt, wear oven gloves to shape bowl. Remove from oven. For stand, use wood screws to attach a 5-inch wood disc to one end of a 1-inch dowel, and a wood plate to opposite end. Apply clear coat; let dry. Use clear weatherproof glue to attach bowl to stand.

Hats Off to the Grad

Hats of all sorts make for a festive graduation party setting. Pick up a variety at garage and estate sales, flea markets, antique shops, and resale stores.

Hip Hat Hooray!

As if tossed up in celebration, hats hanging overhead set the party theme. Use safety pins to attach wide ribbon to the underside of each hat brim. Attach ribbons to a structure using tacks or duct tape.

Topsy-Turvy

Let school colors shine with flowers nestled in straw hats. Invert the hats, line with plastic, and set in plants in school colors. Add faux floral trims or ribbons for added detail.

**Citrus Upside-
Down Cake**
Recipe on page 71

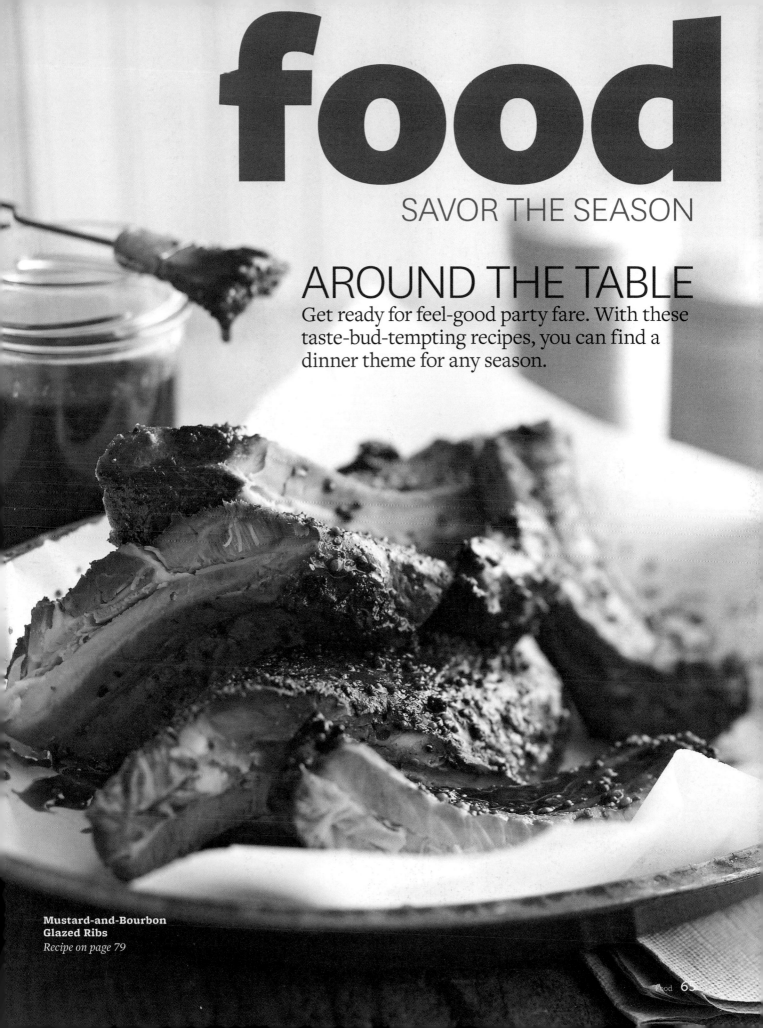

food
SAVOR THE SEASON

AROUND THE TABLE
Get ready for feel-good party fare. With these taste-bud-tempting recipes, you can find a dinner theme for any season.

Mustard-and-Bourbon Glazed Ribs
Recipe on page 79

Celebrate Citrus

Brighten cold days and long nights of winter with peak-season citrus. Grapefruit, oranges, lemons, and limes star in these sweet and savory dishes.

Hint-of-Orange Pancakes with Grapefruit Syrup

Hint-of-Orange Pancakes with Grapefruit Syrup

START TO FINISH 45 minutes
MAKES 6 servings

WHAT YOU NEED
2   medium grapefruit, peeled and sectioned*
1½   cups pure maple syrup
1¾   cups all-purpose flour
2   tablespoons sugar
1   tablespoon baking powder
¼   teaspoon salt
1   egg, lightly beaten
1½   cups milk
3   tablespoons vegetable oil
2   tablespoons orange liqueur or orange juice

WHAT YOU DO
1. For grapefruit syrup, in a medium saucepan combine grapefruit sections and maple syrup. Cook over medium heat just until heated through. Keep warm.
2. In a large bowl whisk together the next four ingredients (through salt). In another bowl whisk together remaining ingredients. Add egg mixture all at once to flour mixture. Stir just until moistened (batter should be slightly lumpy).
3. For each pancake, pour about ¼ cup batter onto a hot, lightly greased griddle or heavy skillet. Spread batter if necessary. Cook over medium heat for 1 to 2 minutes on each side or until pancakes are golden brown, turning pancakes when surfaces are bubbly and edges are slightly dry. Keep warm in a 300°F oven while preparing remaining pancakes.
4. Serve pancakes topped with warm grapefruit syrup.
*Tip To section citrus fruit, cut a thin slice off the top and bottom of the fruit. Slice off the peel from top to bottom, following the curve of the fruit. Holding the fruit over a bowl, use a sharp knife to cut between the membranes and each segment, allowing segments to fall into the bowl.

Shrimp with Peppered Citrus Fruits

Shrimp with Peppered Citrus Fruits

START TO FINISH 30 minutes
MAKES 4 servings

WHAT YOU NEED
1   pound fresh or frozen large shrimp in shells
3   medium clementines or seedless tangerines
¾   cup water
⅓   cup sugar
1   teaspoon whole black peppercorns, coarsely crushed
1   small pink grapefruit
½   teaspoon salt
½   teaspoon freshly ground black pepper
¼   teaspoon ground cumin
1   tablespoon vegetable oil

WHAT YOU DO
1. Thaw shrimp, if frozen. For pepper-citrus sauce, remove 2 or 3 strips of the thin outer peel of one clementine with a vegetable peeler, taking care not to remove the bitter white pith. Place peel in a small saucepan; add water, sugar, and peppercorns. Bring to boiling, stirring to dissolve sugar. Boil gently, uncovered, 15 to 20 minutes or until sauce is reduced to ⅓ cup, stirring occasionally.
2. Meanwhile, peel and devein shrimp, leaving tails intact. Peel and remove white pith from remaining clementines and the grapefruit. Cut grapefruit crosswise into ½-inch slices. Remove seeds and set slices aside. If desired, leave one clementine whole; break remaining clementines into segments.
3. For shrimp, in a large bowl combine salt, ground pepper, and cumin. Add shrimp; toss to coat. In large skillet cook shrimp in hot oil for 3 to 4 minutes or until opaque, turning occasionally. Add clementines and grapefruit. Cover; cook over medium heat 1 minute, turning fruit once. Transfer shrimp and fruit to serving bowl. Pour pepper-citrus sauce over and toss gently to coat.

Food

Citrus Salsa Salmon

Citrus Salsa Salmon

START TO FINISH 30 minutes
MAKES 4 servings

WHAT YOU NEED

4   4- to 5-ounce fresh or frozen
    skinless salmon fillets, ¾ to
    1 inch thick
¼   teaspoon salt
⅛   teaspoon black pepper
¼   cup red jalapeño jelly
2   medium oranges, peeled, seeded,
    and coarsely chopped
1   medium grapefruit, peeled,
    sectioned, and seeded (tip,
    page 67)
1   cup grape or cherry tomatoes,
    halved
    Salad greens (optional)

WHAT YOU DO

1. Thaw salmon, if frozen. Rinse salmon;
pat dry with paper towels.
2. Preheat broiler. Sprinkle salmon with
the salt and pepper. In a small saucepan
melt jelly over low heat. Brush salmon

with 2 tablespoons of the melted jelly.
Set remaining jelly aside.
3. Place salmon on the unheated rack of
a broiler pan. Broil about 4 inches from
heat for 8 to 10 minutes or until fish
begins to flake when tested with a fork.
4. Meanwhile, for citrus salsa, in a
medium bowl combine oranges,
grapefruit, tomatoes, and the remaining
2 tablespoons melted jelly. Season to
taste with additional salt and pepper.
Serve salmon with citrus salsa and, if
desired, salad greens.

Roast Chicken with Fiery Lemon Glaze

PREP 30 minutes
MARINATE 8 hours
ROAST 1 hour 30 minutes at 375°F
STAND 15 minutes
MAKES 8 servings

WHAT YOU NEED

1   4- to 5-pound whole roasting
    chicken

4   to 6 small lemons
¼   cup olive oil
2   tablespoons snipped fresh
    parsley
4   cloves garlic, minced
½   teaspoon salt
½   teaspoon cayenne pepper
½   teaspoon black pepper
2   to 3 small lemons, halved or
    quartered
½   cup honey
½   teaspoon cayenne pepper

WHAT YOU DO

1. Remove giblets from chicken, if
present. Place chicken in a plastic bag set
in a shallow dish. Slice 2 of the lemons;
add to bag. Remove 2 teaspoons zest and
½ cup plus 2 tablespoons juice from
remaining whole lemons. Set zest and
2 tablespoons juice aside.
2. For marinade, in a small bowl combine
the ½ cup lemon juice and the next six
ingredients (through black pepper). Pour
marinade over chicken; turn to coat. Seal
bag. Marinate in the refrigerator 8 to
12 hours, turning occasionally.
3. Preheat oven to 375°F. Let chicken
stand at room temperature 15 minutes.
Drain chicken and lemon slices; discard
marinade, reserve lemon slices. Pull
neck skin to back of chicken and fasten
with a skewer. Tie drumsticks to tail.
Twist wing tips under back.
4. Place chicken, breast side up, on a rack
in a shallow roasting pan. Cover with
reserved lemon slices. Arrange lemon
halves or quarters on rack around chicken.
Roast on lowest rack, uncovered, 1 hour.
5. Meanwhile, for fiery lemon glaze, in a
small saucepan combine the lemon zest,
the remaining 2 tablespoons lemon
juice, the honey, and ½ teaspoon
cayenne pepper. Bring to boiling over
medium heat, stirring occasionally.
Remove from heat and set aside.
6. Cut string between drumsticks and
reposition any lemon slices that have slid
off chicken. Roast 30 to 60 minutes more
or until meat thermometer in thigh
registers 175°F and drumsticks move
easily in their sockets, occasionally
brushing with some of the glaze during
the last 20 minutes of roasting. If lemons
begin to darken, tent loosely with foil.
Remove chicken from oven. Let stand
15 minutes before slicing. Pass
remaining glaze.

Roast Chicken with
Fiery Lemon Glaze

Lemon-Vanilla Tart

Lemon-Vanilla Tart

PREP **40 minutes**
BAKE **13 minutes at 450°F+20 minutes at 350°F**
MAKES **8 servings**

WHAT YOU NEED

1   recipe Tart Pastry
1   recipe Oven-Candied Lemon Slices
2   to 3 lemons
½   cup sugar
1   tablespoon all-purpose flour
2   eggs
¼   cup butter, melted
1   tablespoon vanilla

WHAT YOU DO

1. Prepare Tart Pastry. Preheat oven to 450°F. On a lightly floured surface, use your hands to slightly flatten pastry. Roll pastry into an 11-inch circle. Transfer pastry to a 9-inch tart pan with removable bottom, being careful not to stretch pastry. Press pastry into fluted sides of tart pan. Trim edges even with the pan. Line pastry with a double thickness of foil. Bake 8 minutes. Remove foil. Bake 5 to 6 minutes more or until crust is golden. Cool on wire rack. Reduce oven temperature to 350°F.
2. Meanwhile, remove 4 teaspoons zest and squeeze 6 tablespoons juice from lemons; set aside.
3. In medium bowl combine sugar and flour. Add eggs. Beat with a mixer on medium to high for 3 minutes or until mixture is light in color and slightly thickened. Stir in lemon zest and juice, butter, and vanilla. Pour into pastry shell. Place tart pan on a baking sheet.
4. Bake 20 to 25 minutes or until filling is set and lightly browned. Cool on a wire rack.
5. To serve, remove sides of pan, and top tart with Oven-Candied Lemon Slices.
Tart Pastry In a medium bowl cut ½ cup cold butter into 1¼ cups all-purpose flour until pieces are pea size. Combine 1 beaten egg yolk and 1 tablespoon ice water. Gradually stir yolk mixture into flour mixture. Add 2 to 4 tablespoons additional ice water, 1 tablespoon at a time, until all the dough is moistened. Shape into a ball. If necessary, wrap dough in plastic wrap and chill 30 to 60 minutes or until easy to handle.
Oven-Candied Lemon Slices Line a 15×10-inch baking pan with parchment paper. Cut 2 small lemons crosswise into ⅛- to ¼-inch slices. Arrange lemon slices in a single layer in prepared pan. Sprinkle with ¼ cup sugar. Bake in a 275°F oven 45 to 50 minutes or until lemons are almost dry and covered with sugary glaze. While still warm, loosen lemon slices from paper to prevent sticking.

Citrus Upside-Down Cake

Pictured on page 64.

The combination of vibrant orange, pink grapefruit, and petite clementine slices make an eye-catching arrangement on this upside-down cake.

PREP **30 minutes**
BAKE **45 minutes at 350°F**
COOL **20 minutes**
MAKES **20 servings**

WHAT YOU NEED

1⅓ cups packed brown sugar
½ cup butter, melted
¼ cup water
5 to 6 oranges, grapefruit, and/or clementines, peeled and thinly sliced
2 cups all-purpose flour
2 teaspoons baking powder
½ teaspoon ground cardamom
4 eggs, room temperature
2 cups granulated sugar
1 cup milk
¼ cup butter, cut up

WHAT YOU DO

1. Preheat oven to 350°F. In a medium bowl stir together brown sugar, melted butter, and water until combined; spread evenly on bottom of a 13×9-inch baking pan. Place citrus slices on brown sugar mixture, overlapping as necessary. Set pan aside.
2. In a medium bowl stir together flour, baking powder, and cardamom; set aside. In a large bowl beat eggs with a mixer on high about 4 minutes or until slightly thickened. Gradually add granulated sugar, beating on medium 4 to 5 minutes or until light and fluffy. Add flour mixture; beat on low to medium just until combined (mixture will be thick).
3. In a small saucepan heat and stir milk and ¼ cup butter until butter is melted; add to batter, beating until combined. Carefully pour batter into the prepared pan over citrus slices.
4. Bake about 45 minutes or until a toothpick comes out clean (avoid checking cake too early which could cause it to sink in the center). Cool cake in pan 20 minutes. Loosen sides of cake; invert onto serving platter. Spoon any remaining brown sugar mixture in pan over cake; cool.

Key Lime Pie Tassies

Key Lime Pie Tassies

PREP **25 minutes**
CHILL **30 minutes + 2 hours**
BAKE **30 minutes at 325°F**
COOL **10 minutes**
MAKES **24 servings**

WHAT YOU NEED

½ cup butter, softened
1 3-ounce package cream cheese, softened
1 cup all-purpose flour
¼ cup finely chopped macadamia nuts
5 to 6 Key limes or 2 to 3 Persian limes
2 egg yolks
½ 14-ounce can (⅔ cup) sweetened condensed milk
1 to 2 drops green food coloring (optional)
1 recipe Sweetened Whipped Cream (optional)

WHAT YOU DO

1. In a medium bowl beat butter and cream cheese with a mixer on medium to high until combined. Add flour and macadamia nuts. Beat on low just until combined. Cover and chill 30 to 60 minutes or until dough is easy to handle.

2. Preheat oven to 325°F. Shape dough into 24 balls. Press each ball onto the bottom and up the sides of an ungreased 1¾-inch muffin cup. Bake 20 to 25 minutes or until edges are golden. Cool slightly in pan on a wire rack.
3. Meanwhile, remove ½ teaspoon zest and squeeze ¼ cup juice from limes; set aside. For filling, in a medium bowl beat egg yolks with a whisk. Gradually whisk in sweetened condensed milk. Add lime zest and juice and, if desired, food coloring. Stir just until combined (mixture will thicken slightly).
4. Spoon about 1 tablespoon filling into each pastry cup. Bake about 10 minutes more or until centers are set. Cool tassies in muffin cups 10 minutes. Remove tassies from muffin cups; cool on wire racks. Chill for 2 to 3 hours. If desired, top with Sweetened Whipped Cream.
Sweetened Whipped Cream In a small bowl beat ½ cup heavy cream, 1 tablespoon sugar, and ¼ teaspoon vanilla with a mixer on medium until soft peaks form (tips curl). Makes 1 cup.
To Store Place tassies in a single layer in an airtight container; cover. Store in the refrigerator up to 2 days.

Cinco de Mayo

Take your fiesta outdoors and celebrate this Mexican holiday with grilled pizza and fajitas, a bevy of salsas, a duo of desserts, and an icy rum drink.

Blackened Tomato Salsa

Blackening roma tomatoes under the broiler gives this traditional salsa toasty flavor and ensures just the right consistency for scooping.

PREP **10 minutes**
BROIL **13 minutes**
MAKES **13 servings**

WHAT YOU NEED

1¼ pounds roma tomatoes (about 7)
4   cloves garlic, peeled and halved
2   tablespoons olive oil
6   tablespoons chopped green onions
2   canned chipotle peppers
     in adobo sauce, plus 1 to
     3 teaspoons adobo sauce
2   tablespoons red wine vinegar
     Salt

WHAT YOU DO

1. Preheat broiler. Place tomatoes on a rimmed baking sheet. Broil tomatoes 3 to 4 inches from heat 8 to 10 minutes or until skins are lightly charred; turning once. Add garlic and drizzle with oil; toss to coat. Broil about 5 minutes more or until garlic is softened and tomato skins are blackened. Cool in pan on a wire rack.
2. Transfer tomatoes, garlic, and any juices from pan to a food processor or blender. Add next three ingredients (through vinegar). Cover and process or blend until nearly smooth. Season to taste with salt.
To Store Transfer leftover salsa to an airtight container; cover. Store in the refrigerator up to 1 week or in the freezer up to 3 months.

No-Cook Salsa Verde

START TO FINISH **40 minutes**
MAKES **8 servings**

WHAT YOU NEED

12   ounces fresh tomatillos, husks
     removed, rinsed, and quartered
½   cup fresh cilantro
2   green onions, coarsely chopped
1   fresh jalapeño chile pepper,
     seeded (if desired) and coarsely
     chopped*
½   avocado, seeded and peeled
1   clove garlic
2   tablespoons lime juice
½   teaspoon salt

WHAT YOU DO

1. In a blender or food processor combine all ingredients. Cover and blend or process until smooth. Remove salsa to a bowl. Cover and chill at least 30 minutes or up to 24 hours. Stir before serving.
*Tip Chile peppers contain oils that can irritate skin and eyes. Wear plastic or rubber gloves to work with them.

Spicy Queso Blanco

START TO FINISH **25 minutes**
MAKES **13 servings**

WHAT YOU NEED

8   ounces white American cheese,
     cut into ½-inch pieces*
1   cup half-and-half
4   ounces Monterey Jack cheese,
     shredded (1 cup)
1   4- to 4.5-ounce can diced green
     chiles, drained
¼   cup chopped jarred pickled
     jalapeño slices, plus 2 to
     3 teaspoons of the juice

WHAT YOU DO

1. In a small saucepan combine American cheese and half-and-half.

Cook and stir over medium heat until smooth. Gradually whisk in the Monterey Jack cheese until smooth. Stir in the green chiles and jalapeños with juice. Cook and stir 2 minutes more. The queso will be thin at first, but it thickens quickly as it cools. (To maintain dipping consistency, reheat occasionally or serve in a small slow-cooker or fondue pot.)
*Tip Look for white American cheese at a deli counter.

Pineapple-Cucumber Salsa Pico de Gallo

Sweet-tart pineapple and cooling cucumber bring a fresh burst of flavor to pico de gallo. Serve it with tortilla chips or as a condiment for poultry or fish.

START TO FINISH **20 minutes**
MAKES **12 servings**

WHAT YOU NEED

1   cup finely chopped fresh pineapple
1   cup finely chopped seeded
     English cucumber
½   cup finely chopped orange sweet
     pepper
½   cup finely chopped red onion
½   cup finely snipped fresh cilantro
2   tablespoons lime juice
1   fresh serrano or jalapeño pepper,
     seeded and finely chopped (tip,
     left) (optional)
¼   teaspoon ground cumin
     Salt

WHAT YOU DO

1. In a medium bowl combine first eight ingredients (through cumin). Season to taste with salt. Cover and chill up to 24 hours.

Pineapple-Cucumber
Salsa Pico de Gallo

No-Cook Salsa Verde

Spicy Queso
Blanco

Blackened
Tomato Salsa

Food

Tres Leches
Cake

Triple-Coconut Flan

Tres Leches Cake

PREP 30 minutes
BAKE 20 minutes at 350°F
CHILL 8 hours
MAKES 12 servings

WHAT YOU NEED

5   eggs
1   cup cake flour
1½   teaspoons baking powder
¼   teaspoon salt
⅔   cup granulated sugar
⅓   cup whole milk
1½   teaspoons vanilla
⅓   cup packed brown sugar
      Nonstick baking spray
1   14-ounce can sweetened
      condensed milk
1   12-ounce can evaporated milk
2   cups heavy cream
2   3-inch stick cinnamon (optional)
3   tablespoons powdered sugar
      Quartered fresh strawberries
      (optional)

WHAT YOU DO

1. Separate eggs; allow egg whites and yolks to stand at room temperature 30 minutes. Meanwhile, in an extra-large bowl combine flour, baking powder, and salt. Preheat oven to 350°F.
2. In a large bowl beat egg yolks and granulated sugar with a mixer on high until yolks are pale yellow and doubled in size, about 3 minutes. Add whole milk and vanilla; beat 1 minute more. Pour yolk mixture over flour mixture; fold together with a rubber spatula until combined.
3. Thoroughly wash and dry large bowl and beaters. In clean bowl beat egg whites on medium until soft peaks form (tips curl). Gradually add the brown sugar and continue beating until stiff peaks form (tips stand straight). Gently fold egg whites into the batter just until combined. Spread batter evenly in a greased 3-quart rectangular baking dish.
4. Bake 20 to 25 minutes or until a toothpick comes out clean. Cool in pan on a wire rack.
5. Meanwhile, in a medium saucepan combine the sweetened condensed milk, evaporated milk, ½ cup of the heavy cream, and, if desired, cinnamon sticks. Bring just to boiling over medium-high heat. Reduce heat and simmer gently, uncovered, 15 to 20 minutes or until reduced to 3 cups, stirring constantly. Remove from heat. Pour into a 4-cup measuring cup or small pitcher. Discard cinnamon sticks, if using.
6. Using a paring knife or skewer, pierce the cake all over. Slowly pour half the milk mixture very evenly over the cake, all the way to the edges. Wait 1 minute, then repeat with remaining milk. Let cake cool to room temperature. Cover and chill 8 to 24 hours.
7. To serve, beat the remaining 1½ cups cream and the powdered sugar with a mixer on medium to high until stiff peaks form. Spread whipped cream over cake. If desired, top with strawberries.

Triple-Coconut Flan

PREP 30 minutes
BAKE 45 minutes at 350°F
CHILL 24 hours
MAKES 8 servings

WHAT YOU NEED

½   cup sugar
5   eggs, room temperature
1   cup unsweetened coconut milk
1   cup sweetened condensed milk
½   cup cream of coconut
2   tablespoons coconut-flavor rum,
      such as Malibu, or 1 teaspoon
      coconut extract
¼   teaspoon salt
      Lime zest (optional)

WHAT YOU DO

1. Preheat oven to 350°F. To caramelize sugar, in a heavy 8-inch skillet cook ½ cup sugar over medium-high heat until sugar begins to melt, shaking skillet occasionally to heat sugar evenly. Do not stir. Once the sugar starts to melt, reduce heat to low. Cook about 5 minutes more or until all the sugar is melted and golden, stirring as needed with a wooden spoon. Pour into a 9-inch pie plate, tilting to coat bottom evenly. Let stand 10 minutes.
2. Meanwhile, in a blender or food processor combine the next six ingredients (through salt). Cover and blend or process just until combined.
3. Place the pie plate in a shallow roasting pan. Pour egg custard into pie plate. Pour boiling water into roasting pan to a depth of ½ inch.
4. Bake about 45 minutes or until a knife inserted near center comes out clean. Remove pie plate from water. Cool on a wire rack. Cover and chill 24 to 48 hours.
5. To unmold, loosen edge of flan with a knife, slipping point between flan and side of pie plate. Place an inverted serving platter over pie plate; turn platter and flan over together. If desired, top with lime zest.

Quick Horchata Cocktail

This rum drink is traditionally made by steeping rice and almonds. Purchased rice milk and almond milk speed up the process with equally delicious results.

START TO FINISH 10 minutes
MAKES 10 servings

WHAT YOU NEED

2   tablespoons turbinado (raw)
      sugar (optional)
¼   teaspoon ground cinnamon
      (optional)
1   lime wedge (optional)
2   cups almond milk
2   cups rice milk
¼   cup superfine sugar
1   teaspoon vanilla
½   teaspoon ground cinnamon
1   cup light-color rum
      Ice cubes

WHAT YOU DO

1. If desired, combine turbinado sugar and the ¼ teaspoon cinnamon on a small plate. Rub rims of 10 martini glasses with the lime wedge. Dip rims of glasses into cinnamon-sugar to coat; set aside.
2. In a large pitcher combine next six ingredients (through the ½ teaspoon cinnamon). Stir until sugar is dissolved; add rum.
3. Making one cocktail at a time, in a cocktail shaker shake ½ cup of the almond milk mixture with ice. Strain into glass. If desired, sprinkle with additional ground cinnamon.

Quick Horchata Cocktail

Rack' Em Up

Turn your backyard into a rib shack with this trio of rib recipes and all the fixings—deviled eggs, baked beans, potato salad, and fruit-stuffed watermelon. Yum!

Sweet Tea Swagger

Sweet Tea Swagger

PREP 20 minutes CHILL 2 hours
MAKES 8 servings

WHAT YOU NEED

6   cups water
8   black tea bags, such as Earl Grey
½   cup packed brown sugar
1½   cups dark rum, chilled
¼   cup lime juice
     Ice cubes
2   cups club soda, chilled
     Lime wedges and/or lemon wedges
     Fresh mint sprigs

WHAT YOU DO

1. In a small saucepan bring 3 cups of the water to boiling. Remove from heat. Add tea bags; let steep 10 minutes. Discard tea bags. Transfer tea to a heatproof pitcher.
2. Stir brown sugar into tea until dissolved. Stir in the remaining 3 cups water, rum, and lime juice. Cover and chill 2 to 48 hours.
3. To serve, pour tea into glasses over ice. Slowly pour in club soda; stir gently. Serve with lime wedges and mint.

Cajun Devils

START TO FINISH 25 minutes
MAKES 12 servings

WHAT YOU NEED

12   hard-cooked eggs
⅓   cup mayonnaise
2   tablespoons sweet pickle relish
1   tablespoon barbecue sauce
½   teaspoon salt
¼   teaspoon black pepper
     Dash cayenne pepper
     Snipped fresh parsley (optional)

WHAT YOU DO

1. Halve hard-cooked eggs lengthwise and remove yolks; set whites aside. If desired, set aside one of the yolks for garnish.
2. Place the remaining 11 egg yolks in a small bowl; coarsely mash with a fork. Add next six ingredients (through cayenne); mix well.
3. Spoon or pipe filling into egg white halves. If desired, press reserved yolk through a fine-mesh sieve or grate on fine side of cheese grater; sprinkle grated yolk over stuffed eggs. If desired, garnish with parsley and additional cayenne.

Cajun Devils

Mustard-and-Bourbon Glazed Ribs

Pictured on page 65.

PREP 15 minutes CHILL 1 hour
GRILL 2 hours MAKES 4 servings

WHAT YOU NEED

3   to 3½ pounds pork loin baby back ribs
1½   teaspoons black pepper
¾   teaspoon paprika
½   teaspoon garlic salt or onion salt
8   to 10 oak or hickory wood chunks
⅓   cup brown mustard
⅓   cup bourbon or orange juice
2   tablespoons mild-flavor molasses
2   tablespoons soy sauce
1   to 2 tablespoons packed brown sugar

WHAT YOU DO

1. Trim fat from ribs. Place ribs in a shallow dish. For rub, combine pepper, paprika, and garlic salt. Sprinkle rub evenly over both sides of ribs; rub in with your fingers. Cover and chill in the refrigerator for 1 to 4 hours.
2. At least 1 hour before smoke cooking, soak wood chunks in enough water to cover. Drain before using.
3. In a smoker arrange preheated coals, drained wood chunks, and water pan according to manufacturer's directions. Pour water into pan. Place ribs, bone sides down, on grill rack over water pan. (Or place ribs in a rib rack; place rib rack on grill rack.) Cover and smoke 2 to 2½ hours or until ribs are tender. Add additional coals and water as needed to maintain temperature and moisture.
4. Meanwhile, for sauce, in a small saucepan whisk together the remaining ingredients. Cook and stir until sauce comes to boiling; reduce heat. Simmer, uncovered, about 10 minutes or until sauce reaches desired consistency.
5. Before serving, brush ribs with some of the sauce. Cut ribs into serving-size portions. Pass remaining sauce.

Reggae Baby
Back Ribs

Reggae Baby Back Ribs

PREP 30 minutes MARINATE 8 hours
GRILL 1 hour 30 minutes
MAKES 6 servings

WHAT YOU NEED

4   pounds pork loin back ribs, cut into 6- to 8-rib portions
¼   cup packed brown sugar
2   tablespoons grated fresh ginger
2   teaspoons salt
2   teaspoons lime zest
1   teaspoon ground cumin
½   teaspoon ground cinnamon
½   cup chicken broth
¼   cup dark rum
3   tablespoons lime juice
1   tablespoon vegetable or olive oil
1   small habañero chile pepper, finely chopped*
1   recipe Mango-Guava BBQ Sauce

WHAT YOU DO

1. Trim fat from ribs. For rub, combine the next six ingredients (through cinnamon). Sprinkle rub evenly over both sides of ribs; rub in with your fingers. Place ribs in a large resealable plastic bag; seal bag. Marinate in the refrigerator 8 to 24 hours.
2. For mop sauce, in a medium bowl stir together the next five ingredients (though habañero pepper). Cover and chill 8 to 24 hours.
3. For a charcoal grill, arrange medium-hot coals around a drip pan. Test for medium heat above pan. Place ribs, bone sides down, on grill rack over drip pan. Cover and grill 90 to 105 minutes or until ribs are tender, brushing with mop sauce every 15 to 20 minutes. (For a gas grill, preheat grill. Reduce heat to medium. Adjust for indirect cooking. Place ribs in roasting pan; place pan on grill rack over burner that is off. Grill as directed.)
4. Meanwhile, prepare Mango-Guava BBQ Sauce. About 15 minutes before ribs are done, brush some of the mango sauce over ribs. Pass remaining sauce.
Mango-Guava BBQ Sauce In a small saucepan combine 1⅓ cups chopped mangoes; ⅔ cup packed brown sugar; ⅔ cup chopped onion; ⅓ cup lime juice; ¼ cup olive oil; ¼ cup guava paste; 3 tablespoons honey; 2 tablespoons tomato paste; 2 cloves garlic, minced; and ¾ teaspoon ground cumin. Bring to boiling; reduce heat. Cover and simmer 15 minutes. Cool slightly. Transfer to a food processor or blender. Cover and process or blend until slightly chunky.
***Tip** Chile peppers contain oils that can irritate skin and eyes. Wear plastic or rubber gloves to work with them.

Texas-Style Beef Ribs

When buying beef back ribs, look for slabs with plenty of meat on the bones and between the bones.

PREP 30 minutes
GRILL 2 hours 30 minutes
STAND 1 hour
MAKES 6 servings

WHAT YOU NEED

6   to 8 mesquite or hickory wood chunks
6   pounds beef back ribs (about 12 ribs)
1½   teaspoons salt
1½   teaspoons black pepper
1   cup finely chopped onion
½   cup honey
½   cup ketchup
1   4-ounce can diced green chile peppers
1   tablespoon chili powder
½   teaspoon dry mustard
2   cloves garlic, minced

WHAT YOU DO

1. At least 1 hour before smoke cooking, soak wood chunks in enough water to cover. Drain before using.
2. Trim fat from ribs. Combine salt and black pepper. Sprinkle evenly over ribs; rub in with your fingers.
3. For sauce, in a small saucepan combine the remaining ingredients. Cook and stir over low heat 10 to 15 minutes or until desired consistency.
4. In a smoker arrange preheated coals, drained wood chunks, and water pan according to manufacturer's directions. Pour water into pan. Place ribs, bone sides down, on grill rack over water pan. (Or place ribs in a rib rack and place on grill rack.) Cover and smoke 2½ to 3 hours or until tender, brushing once with sauce during the last 15 minutes of smoking. Add additional coals and water as needed to maintain temperature and moisture. Pass remaining sauce.

Texas-Style Beef Ribs

Five-Bean Bake

Five-Bean Bake

PREP 20 minutes
BAKE 1 hour at 375°F
MAKES 12 servings

WHAT YOU NEED

6   slices bacon
1   cup chopped onion
1   clove garlic, minced
1   15-ounce can red kidney beans, rinsed and drained
1   15-ounce can lima beans, rinsed and drained
1   15-ounce can butter beans, rinsed and drained
1   15-ounce can garbanzo beans (chickpeas), rinsed and drained
1   15-ounce can pork and beans in tomato sauce, undrained
¾   cup ketchup
½   cup molasses
¼   cup packed brown sugar
1   tablespoon yellow mustard
1   tablespoon Worcestershire sauce

WHAT YOU DO

1. Preheat oven to 375°F. In a large skillet cook bacon over medium heat until crisp. Drain on paper towels, reserving 1 tablespoon drippings in skillet. Add onion and garlic to reserved drippings. Cook over medium heat until onion is tender, stirring occasionally.
2. In a large bowl combine onion mixture and remaining ingredients. Transfer bean mixture to a 3-quart rectangular baking dish. Bake, covered, 1 hour. Top with bacon.

Tex-Mex Potato Salad

Potato salad takes a Tex-Mex spin with black beans, corn, and chipotle peppers.

PREP 40 minutes CHILL 6 hours
MAKES 12 servings

WHAT YOU NEED

2   pounds red and/or yellow new potatoes, quartered
¼   teaspoon salt
¾   cup mayonnaise
¾   cup bottled ranch salad dressing
1   canned chipotle chile pepper in adobo sauce, finely chopped
½   teaspoon salt
1   cup thinly sliced celery
⅓   cup chopped onion
6   hard-cooked eggs, coarsely chopped

Tex-Mex Potato Salad

**Stuffed Baby
Watermelon**

1   cup canned black beans, rinsed
     and drained
1   cup frozen corn, thawed
     Tortilla chips

WHAT YOU DO
1. In a large covered saucepan cook
potatoes with the ¼ teaspoon salt in
enough boiling water to cover about
15 minutes or just until potatoes are
tender; drain. Cool slightly.
2. Meanwhile, for dressing, in an
extra-large bowl combine mayonnaise,
ranch dressing, chipotle pepper, and
½ teaspoon salt. Stir in celery and onion.
Add potatoes, eggs, black beans, and
corn; stir gently to coat. Cover and chill
6 to 24 hours. Serve with tortilla chips.

Stuffed Baby
Watermelon

*Baby watermelon is known for its bright
red flesh and fine-textured fruit. You may
substitute any type of melon, and if you
prefer, serve in a large glass bowl instead of
melon halves.*

START TO FINISH **30 minutes**
MAKES **6 servings**

WHAT YOU NEED
1   lime
1   tablespoon honey
1   8-inch baby watermelon (about
     5 pounds) or 7 cups seedless
     watermelon balls or cubes

¾   cup sliced white or yellow peach
     or nectarine
½   cup seedless red grapes, halved
     Lime peel strips (optional)

WHAT YOU DO
1. Remove 1 teaspoon zest and squeeze
2 tablespoons juice from lime. In a large
bowl combine lime zest and juice and
the honey; set aside.
2. Cut baby watermelon in half
crosswise. Using a melon baller, scoop
out flesh (about 7 cups melon balls). Add
watermelon balls to lime mixture. Add
peach and grapes; toss gently to coat.
3. Serve fruit in baby watermelon halves.
If desired, top with lime peel strips.

Spinach Phyllo
Triangles

Indoor Tailgate

Tailgating moves indoors. Enjoy sports and scrumptious snacks on a big screen TV in climate-controlled comfort.

Spinach Phyllo Triangles

PREP 50 minutes   FREEZE 1 hour
BAKE 12 minutes per batch at 375°F
MAKES 18 servings

WHAT YOU NEED
1   10-ounce package frozen chopped spinach
½   cup finely chopped onion
1   clove garlic, minced
1½ cups finely crumbled feta cheese (6 ounces)
½   teaspoon dried oregano, crushed
24 sheets frozen phyllo dough (14×9-inch rectangles), thawed
½   cup butter, melted
    Butter, melted

WHAT YOU DO
1. For filling, cook spinach, onion, and garlic according to spinach package directions. Drain well in a colander. Press spinach mixture with the back of a spoon to remove excess moisture. In a medium bowl combine spinach mixture, cheese, and oregano.
2. Preheat oven to 375°F. Unfold phyllo dough; remove one sheet. (While you work, keep remaining phyllo covered with plastic wrap to prevent it from drying out.) Lightly brush phyllo sheet with some of the ½ cup melted butter. Place another sheet on top; brush with butter.
3. Cut the two layered sheets lengthwise into three strips. Spoon 1 well-rounded teaspoon of the filling about 1 inch from one end of each dough strip. To fold into a triangle, bring a corner over filling so short edge lines up with the side. Continue folding the triangle along the strip to the end. Place on a baking sheet. Repeat with remaining phyllo, ½ cup butter, and filling.
4. Brush triangles with additional melted butter. Bake 12 to 15 minutes or until golden. Serve warm.

Make-ahead directions Prepare as directed through Step 3. Place triangles on baking sheet lined with waxed paper; freeze about 1 hour or until firm. Divide triangles among freezer containers; seal and freeze up to 2 months. To serve, preheat oven to 375°F. Place frozen triangles on a baking sheet; brush with additional melted butter. Bake about 15 minutes or until golden. Serve warm.

Mozzarella Cheese Sticks

PREP 20 minutes   FREEZE 1 hour
COOK 2 minutes per batch
MAKES 12 servings

WHAT YOU NEED
¾   cup all-purpose flour
½   teaspoon salt
½   teaspoon black pepper
2   eggs, lightly beaten
2   tablespoons water
12 mozzarella cheese sticks or one 16-ounce block mozzarella cheese, cut into twelve 4×½-inch sticks
1   cup seasoned fine dry bread crumbs
¼   cup vegetable oil
¾   cup marinara sauce

WHAT YOU DO
1. In a shallow dish stir together flour, salt, and pepper. In another shallow dish combine eggs and the water. Dip cheese sticks in egg mixture, then coat with flour mixture. Dip again in egg mixture, then coat with bread crumbs. Place on a baking sheet. Freeze about 1 hour or until firm.
2. To serve, in a large skillet heat oil over medium heat. Add six frozen cheese sticks; cook 2 to 3 minutes or until golden, turning occasionally. Drain on paper towels. Repeat with the remaining six cheese sticks (add additional oil, if necessary).
3. In a small saucepan heat marinara sauce over medium heat. Serve cheese sticks with warm marinara sauce.

Make-ahead directions Prepare as directed through Step 1. Transfer cheese sticks to a freezer container; seal and freeze up to 1 month.

Mozzarella Cheese Sticks

Food

New Orleans-Style Muffuletta

New Orleans-Style Muffuletta

PREP 20 minutes CHILL 4 hours
MAKES 6 servings

WHAT YOU NEED

½ cup coarsely chopped pitted ripe olives
½ cup chopped pimiento-stuffed green olives
1 tablespoon snipped fresh Italian parsley
2 teaspoons lemon juice
½ teaspoon dried oregano, crushed
1 16-ounce loaf ciabatta bread or French bread
1 tablespoon olive oil
1 clove garlic, minced
6 lettuce leaves
4 ounces thinly sliced salami, pepperoni, or summer sausage
4 ounces thinly sliced cooked ham or turkey
6 ounces thinly sliced provolone, Swiss, or mozzarella cheese
1 to 2 medium tomatoes, thinly sliced

⅛ teaspoon coarse ground black pepper

WHAT YOU DO

1. For olive relish, in a small bowl combine the first five ingredients (through oregano). Cover and chill 4 to 24 hours.
2. Cut bread in half horizontally. Using a spoon, hollow out the inside of the top half, leaving a ¾-inch shell.
3. In a small bowl stir together oil and garlic. Brush bottom half of bread with garlic oil. Layer with lettuce, salami, ham, cheese, and tomatoes. Sprinkle tomatoes with pepper. Stir olive relish; mound on top of tomatoes. Replace top half of bread. Cut into six portions.

Apricot-Curry Meatballs

PREP 35 minutes
BAKE 25 minutes at 375°F
SLOW COOK 3 hours MAKES 36 servings

WHAT YOU NEED

2 eggs, lightly beaten
½ cup fine dry bread crumbs

⅓ cup finely chopped green onions
¼ cup milk
½ teaspoon salt
½ teaspoon black pepper
1 pound ground pork
1 pound ground beef
1 12-ounce jar apricot preserves
⅓ cup soy sauce
¼ cup cider vinegar
4 teaspoons grated fresh ginger
2 teaspoons curry powder

WHAT YOU DO

1. Preheat oven to 375°F. In a bowl combine the first six ingredients (through pepper). Add pork and beef; mix well. Shape into 36 meatballs; place in a shallow baking pan. Bake 25 to 30 minutes or until meatballs are done (160°F). Drain off fat.
2. Transfer meatballs to a 3½- or 4-quart slow cooker. Stir together the remaining ingredients; pour over meatballs.
3. Cover and cook on low for 3 to 4 hours or on high for 1½ to 2 hours. Serve immediately or keep warm, covered, on warm or low up to 2 hours. If desired, top with chopped green onions.

Apricot-Curry Meatballs

Maple-Bacon
Cheesecake Bites

Maple-Bacon Cheesecake Bites

PREP 35 minutes
BAKE 10 minutes at 400°F +
25 minutes at 350°F
CHILL 1 hour
MAKES 24 servings

WHAT YOU NEED

14   slices bacon, cut in half crosswise
½   cup all-purpose flour
2   tablespoons ground toasted pecans*
1   tablespoon sugar
¼   cup butter
1   8-ounce package cream cheese, softened
3   tablespoons butter, softened
2   tablespoons pure maple syrup
1   egg
¼   teaspoon apple pie spice
¼   cup pure maple syrup
¼   cup chopped toasted pecans*

WHAT YOU DO

1. Preheat oven to 400°F. Grease twenty-four 1¾-inch muffin cups. Line a 15×10-inch baking pan with foil. Arrange bacon slices in prepared pan. Bake 8 to 10 minutes or until brown but not crisp. Remove 24 bacon pieces; cool until easy to handle. Bake the remaining bacon 2 to 4 minutes more or until crisp. Drain on paper towels; crumble. Set crumbled bacon aside. Line the sides of each prepared muffin cup with a bacon slice. Reduce heat to 350°F.
2. In a small bowl stir together flour, ground pecans, and sugar. Using a pastry blender, cut in the ¼ cup butter until crumbly. Sprinkle pecan mixture into each bacon-lined muffin cup; press down with fingers. Bake 10 minutes.
3. Meanwhile, for filling, in a medium bowl beat cream cheese, the 3 tablespoons butter, and the 2 tablespoons maple syrup with a mixer on medium until light and fluffy. Beat in egg and apple pie spice, scraping bowl as needed. Stir in crumbled bacon.
4. Spoon filling into partially baked crusts. Bake 15 minutes more or until filling is set. Cool in muffin cups on a wire rack 5 minutes. Carefully remove from muffin cups; cool on wire rack. Cover and chill 1 hour or until firm or up to 24 hours. Before serving, drizzle with the ¼ cup maple syrup and sprinkle with chopped pecans.

Pumpkin Football Cakes

*Tip To toast nuts, preheat oven to 350°F. Spread nuts in a shallow baking pan. Bake 5 to 10 minutes or until lightly browned, shaking pan once or twice to prevent burning. For small amounts of nuts or seeds, toast in a dry skillet over medium heat about 2 minutes or until lightly browned, stirring frequently to prevent burning.

Pumpkin Football Cakes

PREP 30 minutes
BAKE 20 minutes at 350°F
COOL 5 minutes
MAKES 8 servings

WHAT YOU NEED

2   cups all-purpose flour
2   teaspoons ground cinnamon
1½   teaspoons baking powder
1½   teaspoons baking soda
½   teaspoon salt
½   teaspoon ground nutmeg
¼   teaspoon ground cloves
4   eggs, lightly beaten
1   15-ounce can pumpkin
⅔   cup packed brown sugar
⅔   cup granulated sugar
⅓   cup vegetable oil
1   recipe Buttercream Frosting

WHAT YOU DO

1. Preheat oven to 350°F. Lightly grease twelve 5-ounce egg-shape muffin cups; set aside.
2. In a medium bowl stir together the first seven ingredients (through cloves). In a large bowl combine eggs, pumpkin, both sugars, and oil; whisk until smooth. One-third at a time, add flour mixture to pumpkin mixture, stirring just until combined after each addition. Spoon a scant ¼ cup batter into each prepared muffin cup, filling each about half full.*
3. Bake 20 to 22 minutes or until tops spring back when lightly touched. Remove from pans. Cool completely on wire rack. Split cakes horizontally. If necessary, trim tops of cakes to stand flat.
4. Spread frosting over cake half; top with remaining half. Pipe "football laces" on top. Repeat with remaining cakes.
Buttercream Frosting In a large bowl beat ⅓ cup butter, softened, with a mixer on medium until smooth. Gradually add 1½ cups powdered sugar, beating well. Beat in 3 tablespoons milk and 1 teaspoon vanilla. Gradually beat in 1½ to 2 cups additional powdered sugar to reach desired consistency.
*Tip Use any remaining batter to make cupcakes. Line 2½-inch muffin cups with paper bake cups. Fill two-thirds full with batter. Bake 15 minutes at 350°F or until a toothpick comes out clean.

Easy Does It

Crostini

Lemon-Tarragon Cream and Lox

Whisk together ½ cup plain lowfat yogurt and ¼ cup softened tub-style light cream cheese until smooth. Stir in 1 tablespoon snipped fresh chives and 1 teaspoon each snipped fresh tarragon and lemon zest. Spread on 24 toasted slices baguette-style French bread. Slice one 3-ounce package smoked salmon (lox-style) into thin strips; arrange on crostini. Sprinkle with freshly ground black pepper. If desired, top with thin slivers of cucumber and radish and additional snipped chives.

Cannellini Salad

For salad, combine one 15-ounce can cannellini (white kidney) beans, rinsed and drained; ¼ cup quartered grape tomatoes; ¼ cup shredded zucchini or carrot; 2 tablespoons chopped green onion; 2 tablespoons olive oil; 2 teaspoons red wine vinegar; and ½ teaspoon coarse ground mustard. Season with salt and black pepper to taste. Spoon salad on 20 toasted slices baguette-style French bread. If desired, top with fresh thyme.

Blue Cheese, Walnut, and Pear

Place 4 ounces crumbled blue cheese and 2 tablespoons butter in a bowl. Let stand at room temperature for 30 minutes. Mash with a fork to combine cheese and butter. Stir in ¼ cup chopped walnuts and 1 to 2 tablespoons brandy. Preheat broiler. Arrange 16 toasted slices baguette-style French bread on a baking sheet. Core and thinly slice 1 pear; place pear slices on bread. Spoon about 1 tablespoon blue cheese mixture on each crostini. Sprinkle with ½ cup shredded white cheddar or mozzarella cheese. Broil 4 to 5 inches from heat about 2 minutes or until cheese is melted.

Cremini Mushrooms, Sage

In a large skillet cook 3 cloves garlic, minced, in 3 tablespoons butter or olive oil for 1 minute. Add 12 ounces fresh cremini or button mushrooms, sliced or chopped; cook 6 to 8 minutes or until tender and liquid is nearly evaporated, stirring occasionally. Remove skillet from heat; add ⅓ cup dry white wine. Return to heat. Simmer, uncovered, 4 to 5 minutes or until liquid is nearly evaporated. Season with salt and pepper. Spoon mushrooms on 20 toasted slices baguette-style French bread. Sprinkle with snipped fresh sage.

Chicken and Goat Cheese

Cut 6 ounces cooked chicken breast into 24 slices or chunks. Spread 24 toasted slices whole grain baguette-style French bread with 1½ ounces soft goat cheese or reduced fat cream cheese (Neufchâtel). Spoon 3 tablespoons mango chutney on cheese. Top each crostini with 2 or 3 arugula leaves. For each crostini, skewer a dried cherry on a toothpick followed by a piece of chicken; spear onto an arugula-topped bread slice.

LET THE SUN SHINE

summer

FUN TO BE HAD

Let the glorious days of summer inspire the crafter in you. Make projects to spruce up your home indoors and out while discovering new ways to make the season sensational.

Cool Wrap

Wrap cylindrical vases with patterned paper then fill with bright blossoms to make a pretty centerpiece. A trio makes a grand statement along the center of a table. For dining, choose short vases so guests can easily see one another above the blooms.

In Full Bloom

Here's a thrifty way to perk up a plain glass florists vase. Either freehand draw or use a stencil to draw a design on the vase using dimensional crafts paint. Let dry, then paint the vase using multipurpose semigloss spray paint.

Lamp Revamp

Why buy new when used will do? Curvy, decorative, and designed to hold liquid, vintage oil lamp bases make attractive vases. Plus, they're easy to find at flea markets. Group a variety of sizes and shapes on a tabletop or corral them on a tray to form a sweet centerpiece.

Pop's Place

Celebrate Dad's special day with gifts that he'll love using in his creative spaces.

Can Do

Galvanized cans with smooth edges make manly containers for Dad's stuff. To add style, trim each purchased can with a strip of scrapbook paper held in place with double-sided tape and black electrical tape.

Dad's Domain

Whether Dad has a workshop, man cave, or full-fledged sports theatre, this concept works for them all. First decide what you want the letters to spell. Dad's Den? Tom's Workshop? Pop's Place? Once decided, the wood letters can be purchased at a crafts store. Paint the letters if desired or leave them natural. Trace around letters on scrapbook paper that fits the theme of the room; cut out. Use a glue stick to adhere the paper cutouts to the letter fronts. If necessary, put a picture hanger on the back of each letter to attach to the wall.

Fan-Tabulous

Hang dip-dyed fans as a fun spin on
bunting. And, if the weather's hot
this Fourth, keep extra on hand to
fan a breeze. To make one, dip the
end of a plain white fan into dye.
Open and let dry.

Fireworks in the Air

Celebrate Independence Day with tie-dyed and sparkling accents in traditional red, white, and blue.

Summer

Shrimp Sticks

Fireworks skewers add a little razzle-dazzle to cooked shrimp. Aim them toward the center of an ice-filled tray for a showy presentation that guests will oooh and ahhh over.

Chip, Chip Hooray

Arrange appropriately and naturally colorful vegetable chips around a favorite dip. Playful wooden spoons and paper cups wrapped with baker's twine and red key tags add festive flair.

Walls with Wow

Jump into summer by giving walls and furniture graphic detail. Achieve a custom look inexpensively by using a simple stencil treatment.

Pattern Play

Pick your colors and pattern, then get set to transform a room into a showplace.

WHAT YOU'LL NEED

drop cloth	matte top coat
metallic paint for base	1½-inch delicate-surface painters tape
paint roller	
paint tray	matte paint
pencil	4-inch paint tray
stencil adhesive	4 inch roller
stencil	paper towels

WHAT YOU DO

1. Gather supplies as shown in Photo A. Place a drop cloth below wall.

2. Paint the metallic base coat; let dry. Mark center point of the wall for the pattern. Spray stencil back with a light coat of adhesive. Place center of stencil at the center point of the wall and tape into place parallel to ceiling or trim as shown in Photo B.

3. Pour matte paint into paint tray. Saturate roller, then roll onto paper towel as shown in Photo C to remove excess paint before applying to wall.

4. Roll paint over stencil as shown in Photo D. Avoid pressing too hard, but be sure to get good coverage. Redip if necessary. If it needs a second coat, let paint dry to the touch before reapplying. Remove stencil.

5. Be sure paint on stencil and wall is dry, then place stencil for second run, moving down or to the side. Align with stencil registration marks or match the pattern with adjacent stenciled area. Tape into place as shown in Photo E.

6. Repeat Step 3 and roll paint over stencil as shown in Photo F. Repeat Steps 3 through 5 to cover desired wall area.

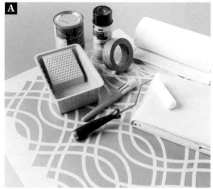

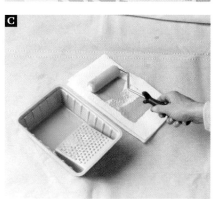

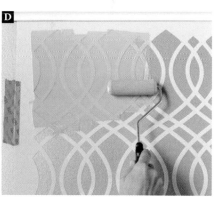

Stenciled and Sentimental

An heirloom or special flea-market find might have emotional value yet little in the way of modern style. Freshen the pieces with stain and add a pattern to bring them up to the current decade.

WHAT YOU'LL NEED
paint stripper, if needed
sander or sanding block
tack cloth
wood conditioner
2 clean lint-free cloths
stain
white crafts paint
foam plate
stencil
stencil adhesive
foam pouncer

WHAT YOU DO
1. Gather your supplies. If necessary, strip any existing paint or finish from the piece following manufacturer's instructions.

2. Sand the piece then wipe with a tack cloth to remove dust. Use a clean cloth to apply one coat of wood conditioner according to manufacturer's instructions.

3. Within two hours of applying the conditioner, stain the table with a cloth, wiping in the direction of the grain. Leave stain on 5 to 15 minutes (test first in an inconspicuous area). Remove excess stain with a clean cloth. Let dry 4 to 6 hours, then apply a second coat.

4. Squeeze a dollop of crafts paint onto a foam plate. Spray stencil adhesive onto the back of the stencil. Press it onto the table. Use the pouncer to apply a thin coat of the paint as shown in Photo A. Remove stencil. Let dry 15 minutes. Reposition the stencil and repeat.

Supporting Cast

Stir up some fun by mixing cement and adding color to create custom garden pots and ornaments.

Planters Aplenty

Attractive, sturdy, and easy to make, these planters lend natural appeal while letting plants shine. Disposable containers, such as small milk cartons and 4- and 6-inch nursery pots, work well as outer molds for pots. Inexpensive reusable plastic tumblers prove fitting as inner molds. Flexible plastic molds work best. Rinse molds and tools thoroughly after use so they can be reused. To estimate the amount of premix needed for a few pots, fill the molds with dry premix then pour it into a plastic tub for mixing. *Note*: Blend enough cement premix—excluding pigment—for several projects then store it in an airtight waterproof container. Scoop out enough premix for each project as needed.

How to Cast Colored Concrete

WHAT YOU'LL NEED

dust mask
waterproof gloves
cement
quartz sand
perlite (available at building supply stores)
pigment
plastic tub and trowel
vegetable oil spray
molds
metal file
sealant
sponge brush

WHAT YOU DO

1. Gather materials to work outdoors, wearing a dust mask and waterproof gloves. Make white-base cement premix with equal parts of white Portland cement, quartz sand, and perlite. Using each mold as a measure, scoop dry mix into a tub and add 2 teaspoons of concrete pigment of your choice into the premix as shown in Photo A.

2. Spray vegetable oil, as shown in Photo B, on the inside of an outer mold and the outside of an inner mold to facilitate unmolding later.

3. Gradually add water to the premix as shown in Photo C. Blend with a plastic trowel until the cement resembles stiff cookie dough and a handful holds its form when squeezed as shown in Photo D.

4. Fill a well-oiled outer mold with the mix to within 1 to 2 inches of the rim. Press an oiled inner mold into the mix until a form with at least ¾-inch-thick walls forms. Level the top of the molded concrete as shown in Photo E.

5. While the cement sets, push down the inner mold and twist it back and forth every 30 minutes. When the cement has set enough to hold its form, remove the inner mold, and make a drainage hole in the bottom of the pot as shown in Photo F.

6. Allow the concrete to set for 24 hours; remove the outer mold. Let the cast concrete set for another 24 hours. Refine edges with a metal file. Brush concrete sealant on the outside and inside of the pot; let dry. Apply a second coat.

Sweet Surround

Accessorize the garden with decorative flair. Octagonal stepping-stone molds form sturdy edgers to frame beautiful blooming plants.

Planter Pick-Me-Ups

Leftover bits of cement fill shell-shape candy molds, yielding 2- to 3-inch ornaments for potted plants. Cast and color concrete using the instructions on page 113. *Tip:* If the cement mix is too runny, add dry premix; if the cement mix is too crumbly, add water.

Heavy Holder of Light

Beautiful indoors or out, this cast two-part candleholder combines a natural look base with polished glass. Two plastic pails—8 and 6 inches in diameter—serve as outer and inner molds for the base of this cast-concrete lantern. Mix white-base cement, and enhance it with white pigment. Fill the large pail about three-fourths full of wet concrete. Press the small mold into the center of the mix until the bowl is hollowed and the bottom is about 1½ inches thick. If necessary, wipe away any excess mix that oozes out along the rim. Every 30 minutes while concrete sets, press down on the inner mold and twist it back and forth to ensure the bowl shape and free the inner mold from the concrete. After several hours, when the concrete has set, remove the inner mold; remove the outer mold after 24 hours. Fashion the bowl into a lantern by adding a 6-inch-diameter glass cylinder, a candle, and sparking recycled glass that has been tumbled for safe handling.

Book Nook

Sweet Sequels

No watering necessary with this book-page bouquet. For the beautiful vibrant flowers in the bouquet, use a watercolor wash (watercolor paint mixed with water) to paint cast-off pages from old novels. To make a flower bouquet, gather an old novel, watercolor, glue, and florists wire. Cut petal shapes from the paper and crinkle to make them pliable, then straighten. To make a petal, pinch the bottom of the cutout piece to shape a curve. Glue petals together one by one. Let dry. Roll back the edges to open the bloom. To finish each flower, insert florists wire into the bottom of the bloom for a stem. Secure with glue.

Lovely Lace

Create conversation at the dinner table with this beautifully aged runner. A discarded book with soft worn pages works best. Lay pages flat on a floor in the length and width for runner. On the back, carefully tape pages together. Use a crafts decorative-edge punch to create a border that suits your style.

Garden Garland

Take a page from the great outdoors with this pretty flower-theme paper garland. Accordion-fold an aged book page. Fold in half and trim the ends into a curve. Repeat with a second page. Using string, tie the two folded pages together at the center, then glue the ends to form a circle. A pearl sticker center adds a pretty touch. Make several flowers for a garland. Thread a needle and string it through the tie on the back side of each flower. Add a dot of glue to keep the flowers in place.

Let It Spin

Treat party guests to playful book-page pinwheels atop cupcakes. Bend a pin at a 90-degree angle with needle-nose pliers. Cut a 4-inch square from a ready-to-recycle book page. Make a diagonal cut from each corner halfway to the center of the square. Roll every other corner to the center. With the pin, poke a hole through all the layers at the center of the pinwheel. Add a drop of glue to the end of a hollow lollipop stick, and push the pin into the stick.

Frame-Up

Repurpose a book with a beautiful cover and damaged pages into a frame for a favorite photo. Using a crafts knife, carefully cut a rectangle from the front of the book. To create a mat, cut a few inside pages into a rectangle a bit smaller than the cover opening. Secure the pages to the cover with glue. Then tape a photo in place. Be creative—choose a photo that relates to the book title!

TIME TO CONCOCT

boo!

GOOD THINGS BREWING

Get in the Halloween spirit with tricks and treats to make fright night hauntingly happy. Games, goodies, glow, and more will make this Halloween unforgettable.

Boo!

Black and White and Eerie All Over

Add a little spookiness to your Halloween party with creepy decorations to set the stage.

Wicked Welcome

Looking for a spirited way to dress up your front entrance? Use classic colors and iconic motifs to conjure up festive friendliness with Halloween spunk—without scaring off neighborhood trick-or-treaters. The patterns for making the banner are on pages 156–157.

Towering Topiaries

Frame your door with fanciful pumpkin topiaries. In a pair of urn planters stack a tower of painted pumpkins secured on a stake, then embellish with fall flowers.

Seasonal Stripes

Guests won't be scared to come knocking with this playful wreath on the door. Simply wrap a foam wreath form with yarn, and add purchased decorations—like a glitzy spider and web.

Boo!

Wrapped in Mystery

Add the perfect finishing touch to happy Halloween decor by wrapping porch columns or yard-light poles with black leaf garland. Simply secure it for the season with duct tape or wire.

Pumpkin Portraits

Inexpensive frames from a crafts store and an artificial pumpkin sliced in half become works of art with creative painting.

Spooky Spiderweb

Weave a web along the front walk to captivate visitors. Strips of black electrical tape transform a sidewalk or stepping-stones into a web of shapely steps.

Creepy Crawlers

For a little silly mayhem, spook friends with a small spider infestation. It's easy to tack the plastic fellows onto pillows propped on a chair or porch swing with a dab of hot glue or a few stitches of black thread.

Sit a Spell

Easy embellishments make this porch ghoulishly cozy. Put a painted pumpkin on display, tie up curtains with orange flagging tape, and let paper lanterns and homemade bats (pattern, page 156) hover over spidery pillows for frightful fun.

Light the Night

Glow sticks make clever lighting concoctions that add to the haunting atmosphere.

Dining Duo

Dim the lights and let these napkin rings shine. When it's time to dine, a simple pair of glow stick bracelets go from place setting to wrist quicker than you can say "boo!"

Creepy Invasion

Chunky glow sticks illuminate spider silhouettes for a spine-chilling sight. Use string to dangle the glow sticks, bend then shake them to illuminate, and use low-temp glue to adhere spiders of all sizes to the free-falling beams of light.

Boo!

Frightful Favors
Party guests and trick-or-treaters alike will do a trick for these clever gift bags. Line clear plastic favor bags with a short stack of glow stick bracelets. Use the rings to hold Halloween candy and tie closed with ribbon.

Links for Lazy Bones

Glow stick bracelets make a gleaming chain in a jiffy. Hung indoors or out, the glowing garland is the perfect perch for a skeleton.

Freaky Frightful Fete

Treat friends to wickedly scrumptious snacks and drinks. No tricks!

Candy Corn Drink

Candy Corn Drink

Start the party with a pitcher of this impressive layered drink. This sweet offering may be sipped by both adults and kids. You might want to double the recipe and make two pitchers.

PREP **20 minutes** CHILL **2 hours**
MAKES **8 servings**

WHAT YOU NEED
1   4-serving-size package lemon-
     flavor gelatin
1   cup boiling water
2   cups mango nectar
3½ cups orange carbonated
     beverage, chilled
1   cup whipping cream
2   tablespoons honey
     Candy corn (optional)

WHAT YOU DO
1. In a large bowl combine gelatin and the boiling water, stirring until gelatin is dissolved. Stir in the mango nectar. Pour mixture into a tall clear 2-quart pitcher. Cover and chill about 2 hours or until thickened but not set. Gently pour* orange carbonated beverage over gelatin layer in pitcher.
2. In a large bowl combine whipping cream and honey. Beat with a mixer on medium or with a large whisk just until stiff peaks form (tips stand straight). Spoon over mixtures in pitcher. If desired, add candy. Before serving, stir to muddle.
***Tip** To ensure that the carbonated beverage stays on top of the gelatin mixture, hold a wooden spoon above the gelatin layer and pour the carbonated beverage over the back of the spoon.

Muddy Swamp Water

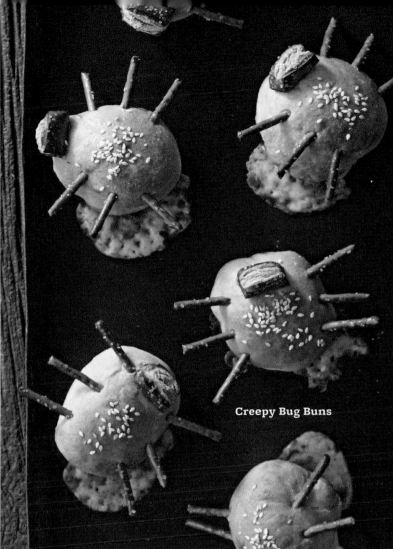

Creepy Bug Buns

Muddy Swamp Water

The simple blend of Irish cream liqueur and chilled cola may look like a stagnant swamp, but it tastes superb.

START TO FINISH 10 minutes
MAKES 10 servings

WHAT YOU NEED
4   12-ounce cans cola, chilled
2   cups Irish cream liqueur
    Ice cubes
    Chocolate-covered coffee beans
    Shaved dark chocolate

WHAT YOU DO
1. In a large pitcher stir together cola and liqueur. Fill a punch bowl with ice; pour drink mixture over ice. Top with coffee beans and shaved dark chocolate.

Creepy Bug Buns

Leave off the pretzels and make these cheese-filled buns year round to serve with soup or as a tasty appetizer.

PREP 30 minutes   RISE 10 minutes
BAKE 15 minutes at 350°F
MAKES 12 servings

WHAT YOU NEED
1¼ cups shredded mozzarella cheese (5 ounces)
1   14.5-ounce can pizza sauce
1   16-ounce package frozen white roll dough (12 rolls), thawed
1   egg white
    Water
    Sesame seeds
36 pretzel sticks
12 pretzel nuggets

WHAT YOU DO
1. Preheat oven to 350°F. Line a baking sheet with parchment paper; set aside.
2. In a small bowl combine mozzarella cheese and ⅓ cup of the pizza sauce.

Using a rolling pin or your fingers, roll or stretch one dinner roll into a 4-inch circle. Spoon a slightly rounded tablespoon of the cheese mixture on dough round. In another small bowl whisk together the egg white and water; brush the edges of the dough circle with egg white mixture. Gather dough edges together and pinch to make a ball. Place, seam side down, on prepared baking sheet. Repeat with the remaining rolls and cheese mixture to make 12 balls.
3. Brush dough balls with egg white mixture; sprinkle with sesame seeds. Halve each pretzel stick. For legs, push three pretzel stick halves into dough on each side of each ball. For head, place a pretzel nugget on top of each ball. Let rise in a warm place 10 minutes. Bake 15 to 18 minutes or until golden. (Bug buns may leak cheese and sauce onto parchment.)
4. Meanwhile, in a small saucepan heat the remaining pizza sauce over medium heat until heated through. Serve warmed pizza sauce with bug buns.

Boo! **129**

Boo!

Graveyard Dip

Graveyard Dip

Guests may be afraid to disturb this vegetable graveyard. Be sure to tell them it's okay to dig in, and to scoop up the hummus dip layered beneath.

PREP 25 minutes
COOK 20 minutes
MAKES 12 servings

WHAT YOU NEED
2   tablespoons vegetable oil
2   medium onions, quartered and thinly sliced
2   tablespoons honey
2   7- to 8-ounce containers roasted red pepper hummus or garlic hummus
1   7- to 8-ounce carton plain low-fat Greek yogurt
1   teaspoon lemon zest
3   cloves garlic, minced
½   cup snipped fresh parsley
¼   cup snipped fresh chives
    Assorted dippers, such as jicama slices, cucumber slices, and tiny pretzels
    Small celery stalks with leaves

WHAT YOU DO
1. In a large saucepan heat oil over medium-low heat. Add onion slices; cook and stir about 20 minutes or until onions are very soft and tender but not brown. Stir in honey. Set aside to cool slightly.
2. Spread one container of the hummus in a 1½-quart shallow oval or rectangular dish. Spoon onions evenly over hummus. Using a rubber spatula, flatten onion layer. Spread remaining container of hummus evenly over onion mixture.
3. In a small bowl combine yogurt, lemon zest, and garlic. Spoon over hummus layer; carefully spread to an even layer. Sprinkle with parsley and chives. If desired, cover and chill up to 4 hours before serving.
4. To serve, stand a few dippers to resemble tombstones. Add pretzels as a gate and wall. Stand celery stalks in one corner of the graveyard to resemble trees. Serve remaining veggies with the dip.

Red Eye Specials

Turn mozzarella balls into eyeballs, stuffed in roma tomatoes.

START TO FINISH 30 minutes
MAKES 30 servings

WHAT YOU NEED
30 small roma tomatoes (about 2 inches long)
⅔   cup purchased pesto
2   6-ounce containers bocconcini (mini fresh mozzarella balls)
30 pitted black olives
2   green onions

WHAT YOU DO
1. Cut tomatoes in half crosswise. Trim the bottom of each half so tomato cup will stand upright. Scoop out insides of tomato with a small spoon. Spoon ½ teaspoon pesto into each tomato cup. Drain bocconcini and cut each piece in half. Use a drinking straw to dent in center of rounded side of each bocconcini. Use the straw to cut out "pupils" from olive halves. Place half a bocconcini in each tomato cup. Place olive in dent for pupil. For eyelashes, using scissors, cut tops of green onions into ¼-inch pieces. Snip green onion top lengthwise in a narrow strip. Use scissors to cut almost to edge of strip. Tuck eyelashes between cheese and tomato with a toothpick.

Here's Lookin' at You

If you like, make these meatballs ahead of time. Store them in a covered container in the refrigerator up to three days.

START TO FINISH 1 hour 15 minutes
MAKES 30 servings

WHAT YOU NEED
8   ounces lean ground beef
1   cup fresh bread crumbs
⅓   cup finely chopped onion
1   egg
3   cloves garlic, minced
2   teaspoons Worcestershire sauce
¼   cup finely chopped onion
3   cloves garlic, minced
¾   teaspoon dried oregano, crushed
½   teaspoon dried basil, crushed
¾   teaspoon salt
½   teaspoon black pepper
2   tablespoons olive oil
¼   cup finely chopped onion
3   cloves garlic, minced
¾   teaspoon dried oregano, crushed
½   teaspoon dried basil, crushed
1   28-ounce can crushed tomatoes in puree
4   2.1-ounce packages baked mini phyllo dough shells (60 shells total)
2   ounces thinly sliced mozzarella
30 pitted black olives, halved lengthwise

WHAT YOU DO

1. In a medium bowl mix together the first 12 ingredients (through pepper). Shape mixture into 60 meatballs.
2. In a large skillet heat oil over medium high heat. Brown meatballs half at a time in hot oil, shaking skillet occasionally to brown evenly. Remove all meatballs to plate. Add the next four ingredients (through ½ teaspoon basil) to skillet; cook and stir 3 to 4 minutes or until onion is tender. Add meatballs and tomatoes. Bring to boiling; reduce heat. Cover and simmer 20 to 25 minutes or until meatballs are done (160°F).
3. Meanwhile, preheat oven to 350°F. Place phyllo shells on baking sheet. Heat in oven 5 to 6 minutes. Place a scant tablespoon of sauce in each phyllo shell. Top with a meatball.
4. For eyeball decoration, cut out sixty ¾-inch circles from sliced mozzarella using a small round cookie cutter. Place one circle of cheese on each meatball. Cut olives in half. Place olive halves on cheese. Return to oven for 1 to 2 minutes or just until cheese begins to soften. Serve warm.

Snake Eyes

These sweet and salty eyeballs are made by stuffing grapes or dried fruit with prosciutto and mascarpone filling.

START TO FINISH **30 minutes**
MAKES **30 servings**

WHAT YOU NEED

30 large black grapes, dried plums or dried figs, halved
1 ounce prosciutto, cut into ½-inch pieces
   Freshly ground black pepper
1 8-ounce container mascarpone cheese
1 tablespoon Amaretto or almond liqueur
2 teaspoons sugar
   Sliced almonds

WHAT YOU DO

1. Trim the rounded end of each grape so grape will stand on plate. If using grapes, scoop out insides of grapes, including any seeds, with a melon baller or small spoon (save trimmings to make pupils). Place one piece of prosciutto inside each grape, plum, or fig half.

Red Eye Specials

Snake Eyes

Here's Lookin' at You

Sprinkle with pepper. In small bowl stir together mascarpone, Amaretto, and sugar.
2. Place cheese mixture in pastry bag fitted with small round tip. (Or transfer mixture to a heavy-duty plastic food storage bag; snip off one corner.) Pipe filling into fruit, mounding into semicircle. Decorate with various trimmings of grapes for pupils or sliced almonds. Chill until ready to serve.

Bright-Idea Lanterns

Draw guests to the door with lantern-like pumpkins atop tall candlesticks. Creative cutouts reveal flickering candle flames inside. To hollow out the pumpkins, cut the opening on what will be the backs of the finished pumpkins and set aside. Scoop out pumpkins. Paint the pumpkins white; let dry. Trace lantern patterns, page 158, enlarging as needed; cut out. Place a pattern on each pumpkin, and trace with a pencil. Cut away the interior sections of the lanterns. Using a paintbrush, paint lanterns black. Let dry. Reattach pumpkin backs using toothpicks. Insert a votive through the opening in each pumpkin. Set pumpkins on tall candlesticks, securing with hot glue.

Pumpkin Panache

Zap traditional pumpkin carving with sensational options.

Bowl Me Over

Using a saw and drill, quick-change pumpkins into pretty, practical lacework vessels that can hold candles, treats, bouquets, or plants. First, cut off the top of each pumpkin; make sure the lower section (bowl) has a straight edge. Scoop out the pumpkin. Cut out the scallop pattern and enlarge to fit each pumpkin diameter. Align the scalloped side of the pattern with the top edge of the bowl; use a pencil to trace scallops onto the pumpkin. Cut along the scalloped line. Using the drill and various size bits, create lacework patterns on each pumpkin.

Webbed Wonders

Embellish painted pumpkins with a mix of spooky shapes. Use crafts nails and strings in contrasting color to form shapely spiderwebs. To make one, trace and enlarge pattern from page 158. Trace pattern onto pumpkin with a pencil. Paint the moon pumpkin black or the bat pumpkin white, leaving shapes unpainted. Hammer crafts nails ¼ inch apart around the edge of the shapes. Make sure nails are slightly above pumpkin surface so string can be wrapped around the nails. For each design, tie string to one nail, then randomly loop the string around the nails to create a web. Finish by looping the string around adjacent nails to outline.

Getting Glitzy

Boost the bling in your landscape with three graduated size painted pumpkins accented with silver-leaf letters that shout out a Halloween greeting. To make the trio, paint stackable pumpkins with flat dark gray latex paint; let dry. Trace the letter patterns, page 157, enlarging as needed; cut out. Trace the patterns onto pumpkins. One letter at a time, brush metal-leaf adhesive inside the outline. Let dry for 15 minutes. Gently place a silver-leaf sheet over the adhesive. Using a soft bristle brush, lightly brush the silver leaf in place until no excess leaf remains. Let dry. Gently brush silver-leaf letters with sealer; let dry. Outline each letter with decorative tacks. Stack the pumpkins.

Scaredy Cakes

Adorn cakes with frightfully yummy spiders, ghosts, and other spooky creations.

Spiderweb Cake
Recipe on page 139

Ghost Cake

Frost the cake with billowy meringue frosting then pipe ghosts on top.

START TO FINISH **1 hour 15 minutes**
MAKES **12 servings**

WHAT YOU NEED

1   package 2-layer-size any flavor cake mix
⅓   cup chocolate-flavor candy coating disks
     Chocolate jimmies
1   recipe Meringue Frosting
     Black edible candy pearls or other tiny black candies

WHAT YOU DO

1. Prepare, bake, and cool cake as directed for 8- or 9-inch round layers.

2. For trees, line a large baking sheet with waxed paper. In a small bowl microwave candy coating disks for 30 seconds. Stir; microwave 20 to 30 seconds more or until completely melted. Place in a heavy resealable plastic bag; snip a small hole in one corner of the bag. On the prepared baking sheet, pipe 7 or 8 small leafless trees, each 2 to 3 inches tall (make them thick so they won't break when hardened). Sprinkle trees with chocolate jimmies before candy coating is set; chill until set.
3. Fill and frost cake layers with Meringue Frosting. For ghosts, spoon frosting into a decorating bag fitted with a large round tip. Pipe mounds on top of cake. Arrange two black candy pearls on each ghost for eyes.
4. To serve, carefully peel trees from waxed paper. Press trees into frosting on sides of cake.

Meringue Frosting In a 3-quart top of a double boiler combine 1½ cups sugar, ⅓ cup cold water, 2 egg whites, and ¼ teaspoon cream of tartar. Beat with a mixer on low 30 seconds. Place pan over boiling water (upper pan should not touch water). Cook, beating constantly with mixer on high, 10 to 13 minutes or until an instant-read thermometer registers 160°F when inserted in frosting, stopping the mixer and quickly scraping bottom and sides of pan every 5 minutes to prevent sticking. Remove pan from heat; add 1 teaspoon vanilla. Beat about 1 minute more or until frosting is fluffy and holds soft peaks.

Boo!

Cauldron
Cupcakes

Cauldron Cupcakes

Tint vanilla pudding deep bright green to resemble a mysterious brew in these chocolaty cupcake cauldrons.

START TO FINISH 1 hour
MAKES 12 servings

WHAT YOU NEED

1   4-serving-size package vanilla pudding and pie filling mix
     Green food coloring
1   cup finely crushed chocolate sandwich cookies with white filling (about 10 cookies)
12   2½-inch chocolate cupcakes
1   cup Chocolate Butter Frosting or canned chocolate frosting
1   tube green decorating gel
     Small green candies, such as candy-coated chocolate pieces, nonpareils, or jimmies
     Black shoestring licorice
1   recipe Cauldron Stirrers

WHAT YOU DO

1. Prepare pudding mix according to package directions, except stir in several drops of green food coloring with the milk until desired color is reached. Chill as directed.

2. Meanwhile, place crushed sandwich cookies in a shallow dish. If necessary, remove paper bake cups from cupcakes. Using a spoon or sharp knife, hollow the center of each cupcake to form a cauldron, leaving ½ inch around edges and about 1 inch on bottoms. Spread sides of cupcakes with chocolate frosting. Holding each cupcake by the top over the dish, sprinkle cookie crumbs around the base to coat. Spread remaining frosting around top rims of cupcakes. Sprinkle with the remaining cookie crumbs; shake off excess.

3. Spoon generous tablespoon green vanilla pudding into the center of each cupcake. Decorate pudding with decorating gel and sprinkle with small green candies. Cut twenty-four 3-inch lengths of licorice. Using two licorice pieces for each cupcake, push the ends of licorice pieces into opposite sides of each cupcake rim to make a handle. Press a Cauldron Stirrer at an angle into each cupcake.

Chocolate Butter Frosting In an extra-large bowl beat ¾ cup butter, softened, with a mixer on medium until smooth. Gradually add 1½ cups powdered sugar and ½ cup unsweetened cocoa powder, beating well. Slowly beat in ⅓ cup milk and 2 teaspoons vanilla. Gradually beat in 6 cups additional powdered sugar. Beat in enough additional milk to reach spreading consistency. (Leftover frosting may be stored in an airtight container in the refrigerator up to 3 days or in the freezer up to 1 month.)

Cauldron Stirrers Set a wire rack over waxed paper. In a small bowl combine ½ cup semisweet chocolate pieces and ½ teaspoon shortening. Microwave 1 to 2 minutes or until melted, stirring every 10 seconds. For each stirrer, place one pretzel stick on the tines of a fork. Spoon melted chocolate over pretzel to coat completely. Place pretzel on rack. Let stand until chocolate is set.

Spiderweb Cake

Here's a sweet cure to arachnophobia. The cutest spiders you'll ever see spin a chocolate web then creep and crawl across the cake top.

PREP 1 hour 15 minutes
COOL 45 minutes
MAKES 12 servings

WHAT YOU NEED

1   package 2-layer-size cake mix
2   recipes Creamy White Frosting (recipe, page 140) or two 16-ounce cans creamy white frosting
     Orange paste food coloring
     Black paste food coloring
2   2½-inch baked cupcakes
1   1¾-inch baked cupcake
3   tiny marshmallows
6   black pearl sprinkles or other tiny black candies
24   black shoestring licorice pieces
     Paste food coloring(s)

WHAT YOU DO

1. Prepare, bake, and cool cake as directed for 8-inch round layers.

2. Tint one recipe of the Creamy White Frosting with orange food coloring.

Spiderweb Cake

Place one cake layer on a serving plate. Spread top of cake with orange frosting. Add second layer; spread top and sides with additional orange frosting. If desired, spoon some of the orange frosting into a decorating bag fitted with a small round tip; pipe a border around bottom of cake. Remove 1 cup of the remaining recipe of frosting and tint with black food coloring.* Spoon black frosting into a decorating bag fitted with a coupler and a small round tip. Pipe frosting in a spiderweb pattern over top and sides of cake.

3. For spiders, cut the rounded tops off two large cupcakes and one mini cupcake. Place one large cupcake top and the mini cupcake top on cake; place the remaining large cupcake top on plate. Change decorating tip on bag of black frosting to a small star tip. Pipe stars of black frosting onto tops of cupcakes to cover completely. For eyes, cut marshmallows in half crosswise; use a small amount of frosting to attach a black candy pearl to each marshmallow half. Place eyes on spider cakes. Attach eight licorice pieces to each spider for legs. For spiders on cake, secure ends of legs in frosting. For spider on plate, use dabs of black frosting to secure legs to plate.

***Tip** To reduce the amount of black paste food coloring, stir in some cocoa powder before tinting the frosting black.

Boo!

Monster Cupcakes

These monster cupcakes are so easy, it's scary. Decorating the cupcakes is a fun activity for a kids' party. Make the three pictured here to offer ideas, then set out the cupcakes, frosting, and decorations to see what young imaginations will create.

START TO FINISH **45 minutes**
MAKES **12 cupcakes**

WHAT YOU NEED

1 recipe Creamy White Frosting or two 16-ounce cans creamy white frosting
  Brown, leaf green, black, orange, and purple paste food colorings*
12 2½-inch cupcakes** in paper bake cups (any flavor)
6 large gumdrops, halved crosswise
  Toasted coconut
  Assorted black candies, such as shoestring licorice and candy-coated sunflower kernels
  Large marshmallows
  Large and/or small gumdrops
  White small oval mints (optional)
  Rolled fruit leather
  Candy circus peanuts, halved crosswise

WHAT YOU DO

1. Divide Creamy White Frosting into five portions; tint with food coloring as follows: one portion mossy green (using brown and leaf green food colorings); a second portion black***; a third portion dark orange, and a fourth portion purple. Use the remaining white frosting for attaching monster parts.

2. Cut the rounded tops off cupcakes (reserve to replace on cupcakes). Spread cut surfaces of cupcakes with some of the black frosting. Place a large gumdrop half in the center on each cupcake.

3. Spread cupcake tops with green, orange, and purple frostings. Place frosted tops over gumdrop halves on cupcakes, tipping each top slightly to form a mouth.

4. Decorate cupcakes using toasted coconut and monster parts as follows: For eyes, attach a small piece of black candy to a slice of marshmallow; insert a small piece of black licorice into bottom of marshmallow slice. Press into cupcake. (Or make eyes from gumdrop pieces and small black candies and/or marshmallow halves, gumdrop pieces, and small black candies.) For teeth, cut marshmallows into pieces or use small white oval mints. For tongues, lay a fruit leather roll flat; fold and press together to make four layers. Use scissors to cut out tongue shapes. Attach candy circus peanut pieces to the fronts of cupcakes for feet.

Creamy White Frosting In a large bowl beat 1 cup shortening, 1½ teaspoons vanilla, and ½ teaspoon almond extract with a mixer on medium for 30 seconds. Gradually add 2 cups powdered sugar, beating well. Add 2 tablespoons milk. Gradually beat in 2 cups additional powdered sugar and 1 to 2 tablespoons additional milk to reach spreading consistency.

*****Tip** Look for special colors of paste food coloring in cake-decorating departments of hobby and crafts stores.

******Tip** If desired, tint cupcake batter bright green or purple. Use about ¼ teaspoon paste food coloring for every 2 cups of batter.

*******Tip** To achieve rich black color without using excessive food coloring, stir 1 to 2 tablespoons unsweetened cocoa powder into the frosting before adding food coloring.

Paranormal Ping Pong

Transparent enough for light to radiate through, table tennis balls are illuminating additions to Halloween happenings.

Eerie Orbs

Set the mood with out-of-the-norm lighting. While white lights would do, alternating orange and purple lights amp up the mystery. To make the string, poke a hole in the center of several table tennis ball labels using an ice pick or awl. Coat each table tennis ball with decoupage medium. Cover with a small piece of cheesecloth as shown in Photo A. Use the paintbrush to smooth cheesecloth onto table tennis ball as shown in Photo B. Paint each orb with random light brushstrokes of black and white acrylic paint as shown in Photos C, D and E; let dry. Gently press onto light string.

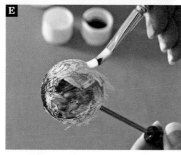

Jack-o'-Lantern Jokers

These silly fellas get their color from using a string of orange lights. No carving necessary, just poke the label area of each table tennis ball with an ice pick or awl. Use a permanent black marking pen to draw faces. Keep in mind how you will display them, with lights inserted at the top or bottom, to determine how to position faces. Slip the table tennis balls onto the lights.

Boo!

Put Your Heads Together

For favors or to add a little boo about the house, these tiny characters make playful Halloween trims. First, carefully poke the label area of table tennis ball with an ice pick or awl. Use a permanent black marking pen to draw faces on several table tennis balls using the photo for inspiration. Place the hole over the plastic "flame" in a battery-operated candle and twist the shape into place.

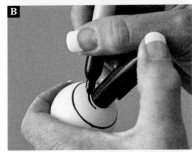

The Eyes Have It

Table-tennis-ball eyes, perched on battery-operated tea candles, add an eerie glow. Display them on time-worn candleholders, in bowls, or other small objects in the uncanny collection. To make one, carefully poke the label area of the table tennis ball with an ice pick or awl. Use a permanent black marking pen to draw the outer iris using a lid, such as one from a large glue stick as shown in Photo A. Trace around the marking pen cap for the pupil as shown in Photo B. Outline a small highlight area on the pupil and color in the surrounding area with black as shown in Photo C. Use a marking pen for desired eye color to shade in the iris as shown in Photo D. Use a darker hue to shade the outer edge as shown in Photo E. Use a red marking pen to draw veins extending from the iris as shown in Photo F. Place the hole over plastic tea candle "wick" and twist eyeball into place.

Boo!

Ghostly Gathering

If you hear a bump in the night, it just might be one of these fearsome fellows. In no time at all you can make a fright of ghosts to watch over your tricks on Halloween eve. For the string, poke a hole in the center of the table tennis ball label using an ice pick or awl; thread onto a wooden skewer. Draw a face on the table tennis ball using a permanent black marking pen. Poke it into a large piece of plastic foam, along with three additional skewers approximately 2 inches from the head skewer. Pour a small amount of fabric stiffener into a bowl and saturate a 12-inch square of cheesecloth as shown in Photo A. Stir the cheesecloth using a skewer as shown in Photo B. Squeeze out the excess fabric stiffener and place the center on the ghost head. Arrange the cheesecloth to hang over the three skewers surrounding the ghost head as shown in Photo C; let dry. Carefully remove the skewers from the ghost and insert a mini light from a light string into the table tennis ball as shown in Photo D.

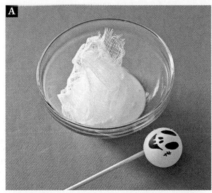

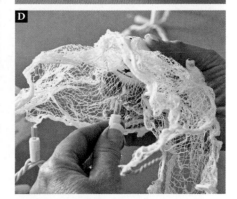

Fun and Games

Entertain party goblins with homemade games that scream with fun.

Witch Boot Toss

Come closer my pretty and join in the game! To keeps the boots upright and open, fill the toes with sand or Epsom salt topped with a short plastic cup. Place the boots on a tray and lay a broom to one side to add to the ambience as well as for sweeping up stray plastic golf balls. Determine a throw line and let the fun begin!

Acting Out

Ghouls and boo-ees love playing this classic with a Halloween twist. Type then print Halloween terms on the blank sides of 8½×11-inch print papers. Mix in terms of the holiday, such as "bat" and "witch," with more difficult ones like "mad scientist" and "walking through a spiderweb." Cut strips apart, fold in half, and place into a holder for drawing. Divide into two teams and use a two-minute timer for each participant. The team with the most right guesses wins!

Mad

Bat

Walking thru a spiderweb

Vampire

Frankenstein

Boo!

Shake It Up

Guests love games when prizes are involved! Wrap up silly Halloween treats like candy bars, spider rings, and pumpkin carving kits. Discount stores are good resources for inexpensive prizes. Wrap each prize and have them accessible when games begin. Have guests sit in a circle and give two people opposite each other a pair of dice and a container. The object is to roll a 31 for Halloween. Each guest rolls once and passes dice to the left. When someone rolls a 31, they take a prize from the pile. When all prizes are gone, guests unwrap their treasures. But don't let them get too excited, because now is the time to steal! Set a timer for 3 minutes and start shaking again. If a 31 is rolled, that player gets to steal any prize to his liking.

Candy Drop

How good is your aim? This might be tougher than you think! Stand up straight and try to drop gumdrops, or other small candies, into milk bottles trimmed with tulle. Use stickers to label the bottles 1, 2, and 3 to vary the points. The player with the most points wins. To capture missed attempts, place a tray or two underneath the bottles.

Boo Bingo

Set aside regular bingo cards and put your computer to use making special Halloween versions of the game. Instead of "bingo" type "ghost" at the top and put a Halloween symbol in the center free spot. Give each player a cup of candy corn to cover called numbers, making sure to have enough to sneak while playing.

Frightful Favors

Mad for Munchies

Bow to your inner scientist with test tube candy
holders. Print out clever labels, such as Witch Warts
or Bat Eyes, inspired by candy colors and shapes.
Trim the labels, adhere to the tubes, and fill with
mini candies.

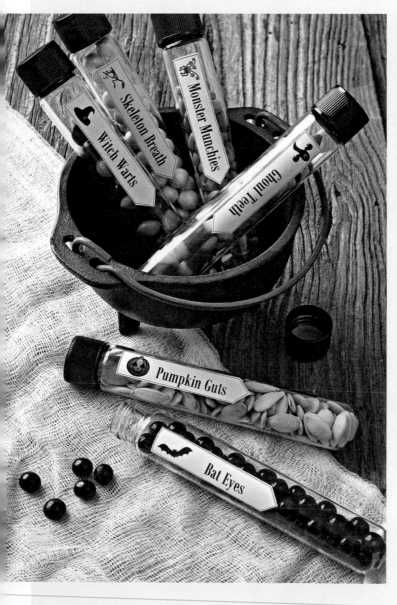

All Tied Up

Fun, festive, and perfect for last-minute favors. Party,
scrapbook, and crafts stores offer an assortment of clear
plastic containers. Make them worthy of the season by
tying filled containers with several patterned Halloween
ribbons. Trim the ends diagonally to finish artfully.

Pleasing Pails

Plastic netting, available in large rolls for little money, adds quick decoration to plain plastic pails. Cut a piece to fit inside the pail, insert it, and fill with candies in Halloween hues.

Clearly Artistic

Set out an assortment of clear glass bottles and permanent black marking pens. Let guests choose a bottle to draw on a design. Have small candies available so guests can choose favorite sweets to fill their vessels.

Second Time Around

Plant your pumpkins, and save the seed packets! These fun envelopes are just the right size to hold a handful of Halloween candy. Line with tissue paper and tuck in wrapped candies.

Jack-o'-Lantern Jars

Clear jars, filled with orange candies of any kind, have sweet appeal. To add character, print shape outlines onto yellow paper; cut out. Use a glue stick to adhere shapes to form jack-o'-lantern faces. Hot-glue short stick snippets and paper leaves to each lid.

Index

CREDITS

Photo Styling
Sue Banker
Doug Samuelson

Photography
Marty Baldwin

Special Thanks To:
For birthday photos,
pages 7 and 10–13.
Ms. Photography
Melissa Scully
Mmscully13@gmail.com